ENTERPRISE ZONES
Greenlining the Inner Cities

Stuart M. Butler

Heinemann Educational Books
London

Heinemann Educational Books Ltd
22 Bedford Square, London WC1B 3HH
LONDON   EDINBURGH   MELBOURNE   AUCKLAND
HONG KONG   SINGAPORE   KUALA LUMPUR   NEW DELHI
IBADAN   NAIROBI   JOHANNESBURG
EXETER (NH)   KINGSTON   PORT OF SPAIN

First published in the United States of America in 1981 by
Universe Books

British Library Cataloguing in Publication Data

Butler, Stuart
    Enterprise zones.
    1. Urban renewal—United States
    I. Title
711'4'0973   HT175
ISBN 0-435-84531-4

Printed in the United States of America

CONTENTS

ACKNOWLEDGMENTS

In writing and preparing this manuscript I received invaluable assistance from my colleagues and friends at The Heritage Foundation in Washington, D.C. In particular, I thank Ed Feulner and Phil Truluck for their understanding, and Don Hall for his help in producing a finished manuscript. In addition I thank the many communities and people across America who made me very welcome and taught me far more about neighborhoods than I could have learned in the finest of universities.

INTRODUCTION

On 20 June 1978, Sir Geoffrey Howe, Member of Parliament and spokesman on economic issues for Britain's then-opposition Conservative party, delivered a speech on the problems of blighted inner-city neighborhoods before a meeting of the Bow Group, one of the leading intellectual societies associated with that party. His choice of venue was singularly appropriate—the Isle of Dogs in the depressed dockland district of London's East End. This part of London is typical of many of England's older ports: Victorian warehouses that were once at the center of the country's trade, but which have now yielded their business to smaller ports specializing in containers and other innovations. It is one of the areas that has experienced the blight and depopulation which can be seen in so many of Britain's cities.

The theme of Sir Geoffrey's speech, however, was much different from the usual discussions concerning the urban problem. Normally, such political speeches fall into one of two categories. Sometimes there is a call for governments to take the plight of the inner cities "more seriously," which is generally just a way of saying that more money should be pumped into them. Or there is a demand that "enough is enough," and no longer should the healthy parts of the country be weakened in a futile attempt to reactivate those areas which are dying for rational economic reasons and should be given decent burial.

But Sir Geoffrey pursued a new line of argument. He suggested that many, perhaps most, of the problems experienced by depressed neighborhoods in central cities were due to the erection of

1

bureaucratic, tax, and other obstacles by the very governments that were seeking to revive these areas. The cumulative effect of these obstacles, he maintained, was that enterprise and social creativity were being stifled in the inner cities—the districts that were once the innovative workshops of the world.

Sir Geoffrey did not confine himself merely to identifying what he saw as the root of the problem. He went on to lay out a radical solution, to which he gave the name "Enterprise Zones." Within these zones, he said, everything possible should be done to maximize economic freedom. Taxation should be reduced and regulation should be cut. No government plan for redevelopment should be imposed on the area, but instead a climate created that would encourage innovation, risk taking and job creation. By so doing, he argued, a process of economic and social experimentation would be set in motion that would restore inner cities to their former role as centers of creativity and opportunity, and break the spiral of decay and depression into which so many have slid.

Although the speech was radical, both in its analysis of the issue and the solution it offered, the thinking behind it was new only within the world of professional politics in Britain. Similar lines of thought and conclusions had been developing in academic and other circles for a number of years, on both sides of the Atlantic. Enterprise Zones were, in effect, a political package emanating from the work of many writers and many projects around the world. For instance, in his speech, Sir Geoffrey paid warm tribute to the thinking of Professor Peter Hall, an authority on urban planning and a former chairman of the Fabian Society, a leading intellectual group in Britain committed to democratic socialism. And in the United States, the writings of Jane Jacobs and others have long emphasized that successful city neighborhoods depend on the encouragement of local entrepreneurs and social organizations, and that these vital elements are all too often snuffed out by the planner with his master plan.

Yet the idea of the Enterprise Zone could be said to have even deeper historical roots than these, at least in the United States. As Frederick Jackson Turner observed in *The Frontier in American History,* the evolution of American institutions and customs was shaped by the need to find effective solutions to unfamiliar and urgent dangers. Old rules rarely applied on the frontier. Daniel Boorstin has shown even more clearly that the success of the towns

2

and cities which grew up alongside the westward expansion was dependent on innovation in all facets of life—from the community laws which allowed societies to function to the inexpensive "balloon frame" houses which sheltered them.* The freedom to experiment, to try new institutions and procedures, was necessary if the pioneers were to deal effectively with both threats and opportunities.

It may be argued that at least part of the problem facing many urban areas today lies in our failure to apply the mechanism explained by Turner and Boorstin to the inner city "frontier." Cities are facing fundamental changes, and yet the measures applied to deal with these changes are enacted in the main by distant governments. We have failed to appreciate that there may be opportunities in the cities themselves, and we have scrupulously avoided giving local forces the chance to seize them. Proponents of the Enterprise Zone aim to provide a climate in which the frontier process can be brought to bear within the city itself.

The Enterprise Zone concept marks another important change in the way the city is viewed. A feeling seems to run through much of modern thinking that cities must necessarily be giant welfare cases—that huge doses of public money will always be needed if they are to survive. Implicit in this approach is the contention that there are really only two policy options. We either can try to lure people and businesses back into the neighborhoods they have deserted, with generous tax concessions, or we can write off these same neighborhoods and allow them to become crime-ridden and blighted museum pieces.

The Enterprise Zone concept would not resist change—change is the lifeblood of cities. The only aspect of urban life that it would consciously try to reestablish would be opportunity. The cities of America and Europe once provided the seedbeds for opportunity. The would-be businessman could try his new idea in an environment conducive to experimentation and risk-taking. A supply of labor was available, together with facilities and institutions to help the enterprise, and a large market was within easy reach. He might

---

*See Daniel Boorstin, *The Americans: The National Experience* (Random House, New York, 1965), parts II and III. As Boorstin notes, the "balloon frame" house was a derisive name given to the unconventional structure by conventional builders. Nevertheless, the design was not only successful for its immediate purpose, but it also became a standard element in the rapid expansion of American cities in the late 19th and early 20th centuries.

3

eventually outgrow the location available to him, and move out of the central city, but the old inner city neighborhood was the first rung on the ladder. And when one entrepreneur left, there would be others to replace him. The city offered the same kind of change for the young, unskilled worker. The wages might be low and the working conditions far from ideal, but at least it was a place to start. He could gain experience, establish a reputation for reliability, and grow with a growing company. For him, it was also the first rung. It is this process of opportunity and upward mobility that has ground to a halt in the inner cities—or rather we have caused it to halt. The Enterprise Zone would try to restart it.

There is nothing about providing opportunities in the city that implies a resistance to change. Cities either adapt to alterations in economic and social patterns or else they die. The point is to facilitate an orderly adjustment, not to oppose it. These changes may occur for many reasons, and they are often sweeping. The towns of Georgetown and Alexandria, which bordered Washington, grew dramatically when it became the seat of government, just as Williamsburg declined when it ceased to be Virginia's capital. Trading patterns have been particularly important as the cause of dramatic changes in the fortunes of cities—witness the growth of Hong Kong and Houston and the decline of Glasgow or the ghost towns of the American West.

Yet it is not this type of change that is being considered in discussions of the so-called urban crisis. We are talking about two other processes. In the first place, there is the general demographic trend that is apparent in all but the most successful cities, namely the flow of skilled, middle income residents from the central cities, and with them the businesses that provided the jobs and were the anchors of the inner city. This flow has led to an erosion of the city tax base, precipitating the financial crises we now face in New York and elsewhere.

There is also a local aspect to these crises. In most American and European cities—even growing ones—there are usually distinct neighborhoods that are caught up in a seemingly irreversible spiral of urban blight. In a purely geographic sense, these districts may seem to have every advantage, and yet they are sinks of desolation and despair. Take the South Bronx in New York, for example. It is centrally located, with good road and subway connections to the fashionable Upper East Side and to the business districts of

4

Manhattan. It also has good rail and river links with the rest of the country and with the Atlantic. A visitor with no knowledge of New York might go there expecting to see a thriving, bustling neighborhood. Instead, of course, he would find himself in perhaps the largest slum in America. The visitor could be forgiven for wondering "Why? There is no reason for this."

Places like the South Bronx lend much to the contention of Sir Geoffrey Howe that we have brought many of our urban problems on ourselves, by frustrating the natural processes of urban adjustment. The Enterprise Zone may be the first step toward an escape from the straitjacket we have imposed on our cities. It would create, within the most depressed sections of the inner cities, areas where there would be a conscious attempt to reduce regulation, and to reduce the stifling burden of tax. The zones would be areas where experiments could take place with the minimum of red tape, and where small enterprises could flourish. Not only would these zones bring the innovative power of the small entrepreneur and the neighborhood group to bear on the depressed areas in which they were established, but they would also be laboratories which would provide tested ideas that might have more general application.

This book will describe the urban crisis that confronts us, and examine the policies that we have been using to meet it. In doing so, it will assess the validity of Howe's argument that much of the crisis is self-imposed. It will then look at some of the thinking and projects from which the Enterprise Zone concept emerged.

The Enterprise Zone is no longer just an idea, however. In both Britain and the United States, versions of the basic concept are being turned into reality, and these developments will be analyzed. It would seem that we may well have a chance to see whether individual creativity will accomplish in the cities what the government has clearly failed to do.

1. WHAT IS WRONG WITH OUR CITIES?

Population Movements

The most immediate factor in the problems facing many of the older cities in America and Europe is a movement of population, both in a regional sense and in terms of changes within metropolitan areas. The 1980 Census indicates a trend that has been observed for some time in the United States, namely the drift of population from the Northeast and Midwest regions to the West and Southwest. While the nation as a whole experienced an 11.4% increase in population between 1970 and 1980, the increases in the older industrial states was more modest. Pennsylvania, for example, recorded a mere 0.2% rise from its 1970 level; Michigan's population grew by 4%; Ohio's by less than 1%. The population of Rhode Island actually declined by 0.4% and that of New York fell by 4%. Some of the gains in western and southwestern states, in contrast, were quite staggering. Nevada led with a 64% increase over the period. The population of Arizona rose by 53%, that of Texas by 26%, and California's population increased by 18%.

According to Jane Newitt, a demographer with the Hudson Institute, the population decline experienced by the Northeast region actually accelerated during the 1970s, making the picture even more gloomy. For the region as a whole, she concluded that the loss rate was 60% higher for the period 1975-79 than for 1970-75.

Worst of all was Massachusetts, where the loss rate more than doubled through the decade.[1]

Some cities within the regions reported even more dramatic population changes than did the states. The northeastern and midwestern states may have registered a small increase in population, but many of their cities suffered a considerable decline in population. New York lost 11% of its population over the last ten years, Chicago lost 12%, Philadelphia 14%, Detroit 21%, Cleveland 24%, and St. Louis 28%. Los Angeles, however, gained 5%, Houston 26%, San Diego 25%, Phoenix 34%, and San Jose 36% since 1970.

Superimposed on this broad demographic pattern has been a migration from the central cities to the suburbs and other nonmetropolitan areas. Detailed census statistics for the period 1970-77 show that for the United States as a whole, the city population fell by 4.6%. The suburban community, however, grew by 12%, and the nonmetropolitan population by 10.7%. This trend is not a purely American phenomenon. Similar changes have been seen in parts of Europe, particularly in Britain. The bustle of the tourist season masks the fact that inner city London lost 16% of its residents between 1966 and 1976. Similarly, the northern industrial city of Manchester saw an 18% decline in its population during the same period, and Glasgow lost 21% of its residents.[2]

Unfortunately for cities on both sides of the Atlantic, this migration is not composed of a convenient cross-section of city residents. The movement consists primarily of middle-income, skilled workers. The remaining city residents, in consequence, show an increasing proportion of unskilled workers, unemployed, and distressed families. Between 1966 and 1971, for instance, only 16% of net migrants from Manchester were semiskilled or unskilled workers, compared with a 35% level among the residual labor force. In 1971, semiskilled and unskilled workers accounted for 23% of the entire work force in Britain.[3]

This polarization between the city population and the residents of other areas is even more evident in the United States, where it is compounded with racial and other factors. Census Bureau figures for 1970-77 show that of the total population below the poverty line in 1977, 38% were living in the major cities (up 4% from 1970), compared with 23% in the suburbs. The proportion of poor in the nonmetropolitan areas, in the meantime, fell by 5% from 1970 to a

8

level of 39% in 1977. Families headed by women have also become more common in the cities, rising from 16% of the city total in 1970 to 21% seven years later—almost double the proportion in the suburbs. The racial polarization is also very clear. By 1977, 55% of black Americans lived in major cities, compared with only 24% of whites.

Various studies by the Census Bureau show clearly that the income gap between city and suburban residents is also widening. Median family income in the central cities dropped from 89% of the suburban level in 1959 to 83% in 1970 and to 79% in 1978. The same trend was evident in per capita income figures. Furthermore, central-city incomes did not keep pace with inflation during the 1970s—suburban incomes did keep ahead.

In the major American cities generally associated with urban problems, the gap was even wider. In New York City, the income of the average central city resident in 1978 was only 64% of that of the suburban resident—down from 71% in 1969. The decline in comparative incomes was even greater in Newark, Baltimore, Cleveland, and Philadelphia.[4] In such cities, about one in five central-city residents was living in poverty by 1978, compared with less than 12% of the nation as a whole.[5] As a consequence of this, welfare payment benefits now constitute a large element of the income of the population in many major cities. 1975 statistics showed that for Boston 32% of total resident income was due to transfer payments. For St. Louis the figure was 28% and for New York 25%.[6] It is most unlikely, given the demographic trends, that there has been any improvement in the last few years.

A 1980 Princeton study by Richard Nathan and James Fossett concluded that there is no evidence to suggest that urban economic trends will alter in the foreseeable future: They suggest rather that the gap between declining and prosperous cities will widen.[7] The authors examined a number of factors that contributed to distress in a city, such as the condition of the housing stock, population losses and poverty levels, and tracked them in sixty major cities from 1960 to 1977. They found that conditions in the most distressed cities fell relative to other cities during the period. Despite the efforts of governments, they noted, the gap became greater. "Quite literally," they concluded, "over the period, the rich got richer and the poor got poorer. Although the final verdict is not in, the available evidence suggests that this gap between rich and poor cities has increased substantially during the seventies, particularly during the first half of the decade."

Nathan and Fossett concede that, in theory, conditions may have improved since 1977, but discount that it is at all probable. The assessment must be a very pessimistic one, they maintain, namely that neither revitalization policies nor other assistance "has had any appreciable impact on any appreciable number of older cities." For this to have changed since 1977, they claim, "would require a major reversal of long term trends of the sort that rarely happens." Even cities that are considered potential candidates for "breaking out" of urban decline show little evidence of doing so. In Baltimore and Boston, for instance, the population loss actually accelerated between 1975 and 1977,[8] and transfer payment income became more important to the cities. According to the study, even the "return-to-the-city" phenomenon is unlikely to have much effect on the downward spiral. Many of the new office buildings that suggest recovery are more than offset by losses elsewhere. And the rehabilitation of residential property evident in many neighborhoods, these authors contend, is insignificant compared with the general decline—they amount only to "pockets of plenty" amid general deterioration.

The Census Bureau appears to have reached a similar view in a study published in 1980. Reviewing the evidence from 1970 to 1978, authors Larry Long and Donald Dahman concluded that the "back-to-the-city" or gentrification movement, "although highly visible and of significance in neighborhoods, [does] not yet appear to be large enough to establish a new trend toward convergence of city and suburban income levels."[9]

It remains to be seen whether gentrification will be as ineffective at arresting urban decline as the evidence suggests. There certainly *appears* to be a dramatic improvement when one walks around Capitol Hill in Washington, Queen Village in Philadelphia, or South End in Boston. But the effect has been very localized. Even the showpiece developments in some cities may not indicate a significant revival. While the Harborplace complex in Baltimore may well be an exciting venture, for instance, one needs to drive only a couple of miles farther out to find totally blighted areas such as Sandtown-Winchester, where once-charming townhouses are now ruins. We should, of course, hope that gentrification and central-city redevelopment will prove to be the harbingers of a general improvement for *all* of a city's residents, but the evidence does not indicate that we should count on it.

Industry and Urban Decline

The population loss suffered by the major cities has been accompanied by changes in the pattern of business development that have added to the distress. On occasion, this has been due to the kind of sudden economic adjustments that have afflicted cities throughout history. Buffalo, for instance, was severely affected by the opening of the St. Lawrence Seaway in 1957. The ships that once docked with grain for the city's mills now steam past, en route for the Atlantic. Almost overnight, Buffalo lost its commercial role; its population declined rapidly, and it slid into the spiral that has made it one of America's most depressed cities. Like all cities that depend heavily on one company or industry, Buffalo prospered while local economic patterns favored it, but received an almost fatal blow when they altered. We may now be witnessing the same process taking place in another one-industry town—Detroit.

But convulsive change of this kind in the economic fortunes of a city is comparatively rare, and is not the primary factor in the economic problems of most cities. Much more important has been the general population movement, which has in turn induced a movement of business. Jobs do follow people to a considerable extent, especially in the service and retail sectors. The larger retail and service firms are of great significance in this process. They tend to lead the way in relocating in response to alterations in the pattern of population: the smaller firms tend to follow.[10] This "anchor" role of larger retail and service firms is extremely important in declining neighborhoods. When a local Sears or Woolco finally pulls out it sends a chill through the entire community. Not only is there an immediate blow to employment in the neighborhood, and to the small businesses that gravitate around a large concern, but it is also a clear signal to companies and potential investors that a solidly based corporation has assessed the area and written it off as hopeless. The economic and psychological impact of the loss of such an anchor can accelerate the process of decline to an alarming degree. And unfortunately, department stores and large retailers are moving out of the poorer urban neighborhoods all over the country.

11

Many city planners have argued that the encouragement of the retailing sector is the key to the economic renaissance of downtown districts, and many cities have poured a great deal of money and effort into rebuilding their retail districts. But retailing needs a solid income base, as well as safe streets, in order to thrive. So it is hardly surprising that planners have found considerable resistance from the retail sector to the thought of moving into poorer downtown areas. Some cities have attempted to provide safety and a strong income base either by upgrading housing in the central district (and moving out the former residents!), or by building convention centers and tourist facilities, in order to use nonresidents as a foundation for the services and retailing sector.

While these approaches clearly have had an impact in many cases, they do seem to result in an oasis of specialized business catering for a narrow range of people (hotels, restaurants, gift shops, etc.), rather than the broad base of service and retail establishments which normally arise in a healthy retail district serving the local community. According to Nathan and Fossett, there is no good reason to believe that these attempts to rebuild inner city retailing have had more than a marginal effect on the cities concerned. Although they agree that such ventures may have had a greater effect during the last two or three years, they feel that, on balance, "much current downtown activity represents economic gentrification—the consolidation of existing activity into a relatively few high rent locations, accompanied by continued decline elsewhere."[11]

The changing pattern of manufacturing cannot be explained quite so easily simply in terms of population trends. There are more complex factors at work than jobs following people. The relative decline of traditional, heavy industries, and their replacement by lighter, technogical industries has had a major effect on the cities. These newer industries are more footloose. They do not need to be near major concentrations of population or natural resources. Nor do they need to be at the heart of transportation networks catering primarily for heavy but low value inputs and products. Ports and railheads are less important than interstates. The central city, therefore, has few significant attractions for such firms; and the high real estate costs and congestion of the major cities are a powerful disincentive. Improvements in road communications across the country, on the other hand, have made the suburbs and small towns very attractive locations.

Manufacturing, with the newer industries in the vanguard, is moving to areas where it can find the best combination of factors of production—where land is cheaper and labor is plentiful and skilled. This means the American South and West in general, and the suburbs and small towns in particular. To an extent, of course, skilled labor is more available outside the central cities because some people will move where they feel the jobs are. In this sense, the demographic changes are a partial result of the changing pattern in manufacturing. But they are probably more a reflection of the desired life-style of the skilled and educated work force. In general, when people become moderately successful, they *want* to move to the suburbs and other parts of the country, even if that means commuting. The migration out of the city is a consequence of the ability of working people to live where they want. It is both a result and a cause of the new pattern of manufacturing.

We can see the manifestations of these trends in manufacturing in almost all of the cities and regions associated with distress. In the old industrial Northeast and Great Lakes regions of the United States some 70% of manufacturing jobs are presently located in the major cities. But if we examine *changes* in manufacturing jobs we see losses in the metropolitan areas and growth elsewhere. Of the 165,000 manufacturing jobs gained by the Great Lakes region between 1966 and 1973, only 25,500 (15.4%) were in the metropolitan areas. In the South, less than 10% of new manufacturing employment is in the major cities.[12]

A similar employment structure can be seen in other industrial countries, such as Britain. The cities that were once the powerhouses of the economy—Glasgow, Manchester, and the other northern cities—are now centers of industrial decline. Shipbuilding, steel, and other heavy industries have contracted or shut down. Today's leading industries are no longer in the inner cities. They thrive in the suburbs and small towns.

The most disturbing trend of all, however, has been the erosion of the *small* business sector in the central cities. The vital role of these small firms will be discussed at length in chapter 3, but it cannot be emphasized enough that small manufacturing, service, and retailing companies are the glue that hold poor neighborhoods together. Small enterprises are not only the most important

13

job-creators in the economy, but they tend to generate the *kind* of employment that is needed in the inner cities—jobs for the young and the unskilled.

Small businesses were once synonymous with inner cities. A small workshop market was a feature of every major city, on both sides of the Atlantic, and small firms were an essential part of every poor, but vigorous, neighborhood. As British urban specialist Peter Hall has pointed out, the workshop was the center of opportunity and new ideas; where both employer and employed had the chance to succeed and move on:

> To put it simply: in former times, the city was always the seedbed for innovation, for new development impulses. Some entrepreneurs grew large; as they did, they not seldom took their businesses out of the city in search of larger scale, rationalized production processes. Others stagnated, or even died; but there were always others to take their place, and again some of those would succeed.[13]

The disappearance of these businesses in recent years has been a signficant factor in the economic and social decay of many inner-city neighborhoods. "We seem," remarks Professor Hall, "to have succeeded in killing off an abnormal proportion, and all too little innovation is occurring to fill the gap."[14] As we shall see, most older cities have managed to remove the key advantages they once offered to small, new businesses, partly out of misguided policies aimed at correcting the financial problems arising from population movements, and partly because of their failure to appreciate the needs and the potential of the small business sector. Unfortunately for these cities, when small companies leave inner-city neighborhoods and are not replaced, the neighborhoods tend to fall apart at the seams.

City Finances

The population and business patterns seen in the older metropolitan areas have brought about financial problems that have added to the momentum of decline. Stated simply, the cost of city functions has risen to meet additional social needs, and the ability of cities to finance these functions has diminished as the tax base has become weaker. As Dickens's Mr. Micawber well understood, this process inevitably leads to misery.

14

As cities have found to their cost, a decline in population does not lead to a proportionate reduction in the demand for services or in the total cost of maintaining the city's infrastructure. Road, subway, sewer, and water systems are largely fixed assets, and the cost of their upkeep is not significantly reduced if the population decreases. In addition, the costs of providing police and fire protection normally rise in neighborhoods undergoing depopulation and abandonment, as vacant buildings and empty streets become local crime centers.

The effect of population changes on the cost of city services was examined in a study published in 1976 by the Urban Institute. The essential results of the study are presented in Table 1.[15]

TABLE 1

Expenditures on Common Functions (1973)

	7 large growing cities	14 large declining cities	New York City
Expenditure per capita	$152	$264	$396
Municipal employees per 1,000 residents	8.7	13.0	13.0
Average monthly wage of employees	$812	$958	$1,115

Per capita expenditures in the Institute's sample of cities that had been declining since 1960 were over 70% higher in 1973 than for the sample of cities that had grown over the same period. When the specific functions were analyzed, the greatest margins of difference found were for police protection (148% higher for the declining cities) and for housing and urban renewal (132% higher—and over 700% higher in the case of New York City).[16] Not only were the municipal expenditures per capita much greater in declining cities, but they have risen faster than the per capita outlays of other local and state governments—which have also been rising as a proportion of the GNP. As George Peterson pointed out in the study:

> Another way of placing city expenditures in perspective is to note that the growth of big city spending per capita during the latter half of the sixties and the early seventies about equalled the rate of total sales growth registered by IBM, one of the premier private market growth companies.[17]

15

While the increase in the demand for protection and social services is an understandable consequence of population decline, leading to a greater cost burden for the remaining residents, it is only a partial explanation of the marked difference in expenditures between growing and declining cities. Another important factor is the existence of a "ratchet" effect, applying to the expenditures and personnel involved in the supply of virtually all city services—not just those where total demand is fairly constant. This ratchet effect has a number of causes. When the number of private sector jobs in a city is falling, there is an enormous pressure on the city government to maintain or even increase manning levels in the public sector. Better to have people on the city payroll providing some services, the argument goes, than to have them on the welfare rolls consuming them. There is also the belief that by providing more services the city can make itself more attractive as a place in which to live or work.

Unfortunately, the practice tends to diverge somewhat from the theory. It is interesting to note from Table 1 that the wages of municipal employees in New York and other declining cities tend to be rather generous compared with those of other cities. They also tend to compare very favorably with private sector workers of comparable skill levels. This might be reasonable if the productivity of such city workers was in line with their level of pay, but this is generally not the case. One needs only to follow a New York City garbage truck for a day to realize very quickly that there is, shall we say, some room for improvements in efficiency.

A primary cause of low productivity among municipal workers in many older cities is arguably the growth of public employee unionization. Unions in cities such as New York have exerted considerable pressure on city governments, under the threat of strike action, in order to win substantial betterments in pay and work practices, and to block attempts to streamline manning levels. In many cities these successes have also included significant increases in fringe benefits and pension rights, whereby the city has won short-term peace by mortgaging the future—thereby incurring enormous future obligations with few, if any, improvements in current efficiency.

Even when manning cuts have been accepted by public employee unions, they have generally tried to achieve these reductions through natural attrition. Not only is this an expensive

16

way of reducing manning levels, since the reduction is offset by expenditures on pension commitments, but it is also very haphazard; it rarely allows an effective cost-cutting reorganization to take place. Whenever cost reductions are achieved, cuts in personnel and unnecessary overhead expenditures are invariably the last things that are accomplished. Although the frequency of garbage pickups may be cut, it is seldom that the size of the truck crew will be reduced or work methods will be less wasteful.

While they are faced on the one side with the problem of reducing municipal expenditures, declining cities must also contend with revenue implications of migration. The movement of middle-income residents out of the city has obvious effects on the revenues arising from sales and other spending-related taxes, but the most damaging effects are a result of the heavy reliance of larger cities on property taxes as the principal form of finance. The property tax accounts for almost two-thirds of all locally collected general revenues and about three-quarters of local taxes.

The yield from property tax tends to hold more firmly than most other taxes during a period of inflation, since housing values usually rise faster than other prices. But in rapidly declining cities this is normally offset by other factors that depress the property tax base. Business closures weaken the nonresidential tax income. But as the Urban Institute has noted, the most depressing effect is due simply to the fall in the demand for housing:

> No city can withstand population losses of more than 20 percent in the space of 13 years, as has happened in Buffalo, Cleveland, Pittsburgh and St. Louis, without suffering a decline in the demand for the city's standing stock of housing. This is reflected in lower housing prices. The cities in our sample with the worst population declines enjoyed only marginal increases in average housing prices during the period which was, for most of the country, one of rampant house price inflation.[18]

Table 2 presents further findings of the Urban Institute study and indicates the relationship between the property tax base and city expenditures in the municipalities examined.[19]

In the growing cities, revenues have benefited from the central role of the property tax in municipal finance, but in declining cities exactly the opposite has been true. The study estimated that over the decade 1961-71, each 1% alteration in a city's rate of population

TABLE 2

Expenditures and Property Tax Base Growth
(Selected Cities, 1965-73)

Declining Cities	Growth in Expenditure (City Government Only) (percent)	True Growth of Property Tax Value (percent)
Baltimore	172	33
Buffalo	135	21
Cleveland	67	36
Detroit	129	14
Newark	135	2
Philadelphia	130	70
New York City	186	68
Growing Cities		
Houston	118	136
Memphis	65	76
Phoenix	166	251
Portland, Oregon	141	172
San Diego	126	167

change (growth or decline) was accompanied by a 1.3% change in the per capita value of the property tax base. The income level of residents was also found to have on the property tax base: For the same period, a 1% change in per capita income growth was associated with no less than a 2.3% change in per capita property values.[20] Thus, the trend in most declining cities of middle and upper income residents moving to other areas is particularly damaging to the foundation of the tax revenue of the cities.

Declining cities are thus caught between two opposing forces. They experience a growing demand for certain services, simply because they are declining. And yet they are also faced with the dual problem of streamlining city services while the tax base to finance those services gets weaker.

What Should Be Done?

It is one thing to recognize that the older, major cities have some very severe problems, but quite another to agree on what can and should be done. The conventional wisdom, until perhaps a few

18

years ago, was that the demographic changes that were taking place were likely to decelerate and cease—or even reverse as a new equilibrium was reached. In addition, the thinking then went, a good deal of the migration was due to the age and disrepair of the infrastructure and housing stock of the cities. With the correct application of sufficient money this could presumably be rectified and we would be on the road to urban recovery.

One would have to be a supreme optimist to hold that view today. Despite the infusion of billions of dollars, the migration continues remorselessly and the plight of the central cities becomes ever more dire. Furthermore, the population movements seem almost unrelated to the amount of money spent in a city, suggesting that the quantity of money needed to influence population patterns may be staggering. Nor is the problem limited to the United States. Many European cities are going through the same traumatic adjustment. The older cities are clearly in the grip of powerful economic and social forces against which the efforts of government seem quite ineffective.

Many people would argue that we should not even be trying to stop or slow down this process, and that it is merely a reflection of a change in life-style and the desire of people to exploit new opportunities open to them. President Carter's Commission for a National Agenda argued in its controversial urban report that a systematic attempt to reverse a natural adjustment is to thwart people in favor of places. If we did not want people to move to the Southwest, why did we build interstate highways and pour government resources into enabling development of these new regions to go ahead? It is a compelling argument. People are demonstrating a pronounced desire to move to where new opportunities exist and in general to live in places other than the central cities. When people are allowed to pursue these desires, it benefits the nation as a whole.

The contention that we should not interfere with this natural pattern of change is not to say that cities are finished in some historical sense, but simply that they are altering. It may be that the demographic pattern may change in years to come, or even reverse, leading to a new age for cities. We do not know. Yet any student of history would find it difficult to believe that older cities as a whole are in some inexorable decline. They may, as a whole, become smaller, and perform different functions for a different group of residents. But, as columnist George Will recently observed, "Cities are permanent; their characters and functions are not. There will always be a London, but there have been many Londons."[21]

It would seem to many that it is but a short step from the position that population movements are necessary and healthy to the conclusion that they should be assisted by government. The Commission for a National Agenda took the view that it should be the role of government to facilitate migration, while giving assistance to communities undergoing painful transition:

> A people-to-jobs strategy should be crafted with priority over, but in concert with, the jobs-to-people strategy that serves as a major theme in current urban policy. Greater emphasis on developing a policy of assisted migration would help underemployed and displaced workers who wish to migrate to locations of long-term economic growth. This option is especially necessary for residents of severely distressed, older industrial cities facing relatively permanent contraction of their economic and population bases.[22]

Despite the furor over the Commission report, the idea of "planned shrinkage" combined with relocation assistance has attained a position of some respectability. Even *The New York Times* is no longer averse to talking in such terms. In an editorial entitled "Helping the Poor Escape," for instance, the newspaper gave strong support to the idea of helping the poorer residents of distressed cities move to areas where jobs are available, including measures such as reforming welfare and housing policies which currently reduce mobility. By removing obstacles that now exist, the *Times* went on, we would unlock the invisible gates of the ghetto and allow the poor to head for the opportunities that exist elsewhere: "Labor force mobility has long been a characteristic of, indeed essential to, a healthy economy. People with the confidence and means to do so are free to act out the traditional urge to move on. Greener pastures: it's not only right, it's the American Way." [23]

The New York Times may pride itself in presenting all the news that's fit for print, but the reactions of many urban leaders to the idea of planned shrinkage is quite unprintable. Nevertheless, there does seem to be a growing, albeit unenthusiastic, acceptance among city officials that this is part of the only viable strategy for older urban areas. Some have even managed to put a brave face on it, like Buffalo Comptroller Robert Whelan. In a speech in 1977, after that city regained its bond rating, he took the view that, "If we hold through this period of shrinkage; if we can wait until our population reaches bottom; and if we can succeed in developing things that are part of the economic base ... then we are going to have a healthy, midsized city." [24]

There is a good deal of common sense to this attitude. Making fundamental social changes less painful is generally a more sensible and successful policy than trying to oppose change. But there is a danger. Sanitized terms such as "planned shrinkage" or "orderly disinvestment" may mask a policy of total neglect, on the assumption that certain parts of a city should be written off—in effect, that they should be locked up and the key thrown away.

Such a policy would constitute the greatest folly imaginable. The assumption that some districts of major cities are by nature jungles of hopelessness guarantees that they will stay that way. Political redlining is far more destructive than the commercial variety, and leads to the destruction of whatever latent strength a neighborhood has, condemning it to becoming a welfare ghetto, riddled with despair and crime.

The short-sightedness of the strategy of planned abandonment has been well explained by urban columnist Neal Peirce:

> When we tour New York's supposedly hopeless neighborhoods, the wrong-headedness of planned shrinkage is immediately evident. Many of the buildings are architectural gems. Most have sturdy, thick brick walls that would cost immense sums to build now....They cry out for restoration not abandonment. The capital investment that would be lost in the abandonment of whole neighborhoods is staggering. Cheek-to-jowl with troubled residential blocks are schools, hospitals, firehouses and police stations. Water, sewer, and electric lines are in place. Many of the neighborhoods are on subway lines a few minutes from Manhattan, downtown Brooklyn and other employment centers vital to low income workers. To recreate this massive infrastructure would cost billions of dollars. [25]

As Peirce emphasizes, it is a fundamental error to assume that most distressed neighborhoods are somehow devoid of any assets or potential, and that nothing would be lost in closing them down—even if this were possible. Yet, as we shall see later, many government policies have not merely failed to build on the human and other capital in these "hopeless" areas, but have actually had the effect of reducing it. Often the sum total of government strategy has consisted of ruining neighborhoods with one set of policies and then pouring vast amounts of money into the same neighborhoods in a futile effort to revive them.

What we must do in the inner cities is to remove the obstacles that we have erected, obstacles that have transformed the inner cities from centers of opportunity into blighted sinks of hopelessness. Revitalizing neighborhoods does not mean physically rebuilding them, nor does it mean taking resources away from efficient uses and putting them to inefficient use in bad neighborhoods. What it should mean is a strategy aimed at building a *climate, in which people are encouraged to use the latent strengths of an area to take advantage of opportunities that actually exist. This approach to revitalization does not run counter to the natural process of change that mus*t take place in a nation, which necessarily alters the nature of many of its cities. Seeking to create an environment in which depressed parts of the country have an incentive to realize their own potential is not in any way contradictory to a policy of accepting change.

NOTES

1. *Wall Street Journal,* 9 December 1980.
2. *Policy for the Inner Cities* (HMSO, London, 1977), p. 2.
3. *Ibid.*
4. See *The President's National Urban Policy Report* (U.S. Department of Housing and Urban Development, Washington, D.C., 1980).
5. The Census Bureau considered a family of four to be poor in 1978 if its cash income was less than $6,662.
6. Testimony before the Senate Finance Committee by Donna Shalala, assistant secretary for policy development, Department of Housing and Urban Development, *Congressional Record,* 10 May 1979, p. 2224.
7. Richard Nathan and James Fossett, *The Prospects for Urban Revival* (Princeton University, 1980).
8. It should be pointed out, however, that the 1980 Census indicates that the 3.5% loss of population by Baltimore over the decade was the lowest of any major eastern or midwestern city. During the same period, Boston contracted by 12.3%.
9. *Washington Post,* 28 May 1980.
10. For a study of this process in the Great Lakes Region, see Donald Steinnes, *The Importance of Small Business in the Urban Development and Revitalization of Central Cities in the Region* (University of Minnesota, 1979, unpublished). The importance of major retail stores as anchors in suburban malls is well known.
11. Nathan and Fossett, *Prospects,* p. 19.

12. *Stimulating the Economy of the Great Lakes States* (Academy for Contemporary Problems, Columbus, Ohio, 1977), p. 19.
13. Speech to the Royal Town Planning Institute, Chester, England, 15 June 1977.
14. *Ibid.*
15. George Peterson, "Finance," in William Gorham and Nathan Glazer (eds.), *The Urban Predicament* (The Urban Institute, Washington, D.C., 1976), p. 48. The cities in the sample were: *growing* (i.e., gained population between 1960 and 1973)—Honolulu, Houston, Jacksonville, Memphis, Phoenix, San Antonio, and San Diego; *declining* (i.e., lost population)—Baltimore, Boston, Buffalo, Chicago, Cincinnati, Cleveland, Detroit, Milwaukee, New Orleans, Philadelphia, Pittsburgh, St. Louis, San Francisco, and Seattle. New York City, also declining, is listed separately.
16. *Ibid.*, p. 49.
17. *Ibid.*, p. 41.
18. *Ibid.*, p. 54. According to this study, between 1966 and 1971 the average value of single family houses sold in Buffalo, Cleveland, Pittsburgh and St. Louis—each of which lost more than 20% of its population between 1960 and 1973—increased by an average of just 0.03%. In the cities that grew over the period 1966-1971, the sale price of such housing increased by 48%.
19. *Ibid.*, p. 52.
20. *Ibid.*, p. 55.
21. *Washington Post*, 1 January 1981.
22. President's Commission for a National Agenda for the Eighties, *Urban America in the Eighties* (USGPO, Washington, D.C., 1980), pp. 106-107.
23. *The New York Times*, 8 December 1980.
24. *Time*, 8 August 1977, p. 80.
25. *Washington Post*, 30 March 1977.

2. THE RESPONSE OF GOVERNMENT

City Finances

It is abundantly clear from even a cursory examination of urban trends that whatever government *is* doing in the inner cities it is not bringing about a general revival. It could be, of course, that without the actions that have been taken the situation would be a great deal worse. Yet, while certain policies have clearly led to improvements in some neighborhoods, it can be argued that other policies have actually accelerated decline, because they have been rooted in a basic misunderstanding of the nature of neighborhoods. In other cases, such as the complex issue of city finance, political pressures have encouraged officials to take actions that yield short-term benefits while weakening the fabric of the city.

When ordinary people find that their expenditures exceed their income they have a number of alternatives. They can try to boost their income; they can borrow on the assumption that the future will be more favorable; or they can reduce their expenditures. They can also go bankrupt.

Cities have tried all these options with varying degrees of failure. Attempts in recent years to balance the books through tax increases have rarely been very successful, and have often turned out to be counterproductive. There are a number of reasons for this. Raising taxes on property makes the city even less attractive and increases the exodus of people and businesses. This problem is aggravated in the older cities of the United States because of the pattern of taxing boundaries. Typically, the poorer sections of metropolitan areas are in one jurisdiction (the city), and the suburbs are in another. While it is common for expanding cities in the South and West to expand their taxable borders it is virtually impossible for cities in the East to do so. In theory, agreements can be reached between cities and their suburbs in separate jurisdictions to achieve some form of equity, but such agreements are very difficult to negotiate. A contract is not easy to achieve when one side is asked to give up income while receiving no direct benefit in return.

The existence of these rigid tax borders means that an increase in city taxes will increase the differential between a city and its suburbs. Thus, businesses and residents of the city will find it more attractive to be in the suburbs, and some will move. If this happens, the tax base erodes, and the greater the future tax increases must be—increasing the differential and hence the incentive for residents to move.

We can see this frustrating situation in most declining cities of the East and Great Lakes regions. In Washington, D.C., for example, taxes on business have been rising sharply in recent years, while those in the Virginia and Maryland suburbs have remained fairly stable or have declined. This has encouraged companies to move from the city to what have become booming new business districts in the suburbs, and it has also led to professional and technical workers moving out of the city, causing a further erosion of the tax base. Increases in personal property taxes and other tax costs associated with living in Washington have also caused professionals to move their residence to the suburbs, even if they continue to work in the city. Between 1970 and 1978 the proportion of professional, technical, and managerial positions in Washington held by non-District residents rose from 35% to 40%.[1]

Many cities have experimented both with alternatives to the traditional property tax and with ways of extracting tax revenue from nonresident workers. A city sales tax can help, but tends to have only a limited impact on nonresidents. It adds to the cost of living in the city and hurts already hard-pressed city retailers who are trying to compete with suburban shopping centers. A dramatic example of this problem was seen in the case of the ill-fated gasoline tax of 6 cents imposed by Washington, D.C. Not only did nonresident workers react by reducing their purchases in the city, but even residents began to cross the border to fill their tanks. District sales plummeted, gas stations closed down, and eventually the tax had to be repealed.

Commuter payroll taxes have also been very controversial and often counterproductive, even though such taxes may seem a reasonable way of charging people who use the facilities of the city. The problem is, as the Urban Institute explains:

> For all its one-time benefits...a commuter tax cannot slow the long-term deterioration in the central city tax base unless jobs leave the city at a less rapid pace than do households. At best, this is a precarious hope. Although the evidence on job decentralization is somewhat mixed, over extended periods of time jobs and people seem to be deserting the central cities in about equal measure. Thus a tax on downtown jobs is likely to provide no more long-run revenue growth than a tax on downtown property or a tax on downtown retail sales.[2]

Some cities have sought to break out of the property tax spiral by providing property tax abatement for selected firms that agree to construct buildings in the city. The assumption is that if abatement lasting twenty or thirty years entices a company that would otherwise not come to the city, nothing is lost—and there may be much to gain. Other companies may stay in or move to the area, because the abated company is there, and these will contribute to the tax base. The existence of these strong downtown facilities could help to reduce or reverse the migration of professionals.

The final conclusion on tax abatement is still to be made. Some cities argue that it has been responsible for major redevelopment, and that the sites that were given abatement would have lain vacant otherwise, producing no tax income and reducing the value of neighboring property. Yet there is also strong opposition to the policy by the residents of other cities, who maintain that major corporations are obtaining benefits that other taxpayers must pay for. While this is a doubtful argument in the short term, since there is normally little or no activity on the sites chosen, there is some merit in the contention that the city is writing off the future. If conditions in the older cities do improve for reasons other than abatement itself, then St. Louis, Boston, and many other municipalities will discover that in their midst they have large, profitable corporations that are gaining from the general improvement but are contributing nothing to property tax revenues.

The problems cities face in attempting to increase revenues solely from sources within their tax jurisdiction, together with equity arguments, have strengthened the pressure for greater sharing of tax revenues between jurisdictions that fall within the same metropolitan area. Older cities in the Northeast, however, contend that a regional imbalance must also be corrected. They claim that the net effect of federal tax policy has been to drain money from the East and Midwest, where it is sorely needed, and to funnel it via Washington to regions of the country that do not need it for development.

A number of studies have given support to this contention. The *National Journal*, for example, has analyzed the net flow of federal dollars by state over the period 1975-79. While the differences have narrowed a little over this period, the pattern is still very clear. In the Northeast, in 1979, the federal government spent 97 cents in the region for every dollar it collected in taxes. In the Midwest, the region received only 79 cents for every dollar raised. The South, however, received $1.12 for each dollar in taxes, and the West $1.05. In the case of the Great Lakes states, this translated into a net outflow of over $27 billion.[3]

These kinds of cost-benefit analyses are, of course, open to challenge. Defense expenditures in the Midwest and West, for example, presumably benefit the eastern cities even though the money is not spent there. Similarly, government-assisted development of natural resources in the West means a less-expensive supply of raw materials for other regions. Nevertheless, the disparity assisted the drive to give direct aid to certain areas, by way of the Johnson "Great Society" programs and later in the form of general revenue sharing enacted under President Nixon.

As Table 3 indicates, finance from outside the city had become a major element in the revenue of declining cities by the early 1970s, accounting for over two-thirds of the revenue growth over the period 1965-73 in the case of Baltimore.[4]

Unfortunately, Parkinson's Law seems to apply to city finance, in that whenever new sources of finance are added to the budget, additional financial commitments always seem to appear to absorb (or exceed) them. These commitments also tend to be permanent in nature. So when the economic situation in the mid-1970s led to a slowdown in intergovernmental assistance, many cities found themselves in severe difficulties.

27

TABLE 3

Sources of Selected Cities Revenue Growth, 1965-73
(Percentage of Total Revenue Growth)

	Local Revenue	State and Federal Aid	Net Annual Borrowing
Declining Cities			
Baltimore	29	68	3
Buffalo	29	62	9
Detroit	44	48	8
New York	37	55	8
Growing Cities			
Atlanta	56	18	26
Houston	58	28	14
San Diego	57	41	2

Since cuts in regular services have proved extremely difficult to achieve, many cities have taken the easier option of reducing expenditures on the maintenance of basic infrastructure—roads, sewers, bridges, and so on. The term "deferred maintenance" has now crept into the municipal vocabulary, meaning simply the decision to put off work needed to keep the fabric of a city in full working order.

There are vivid examples of the consequences of deferred maintenance. Half of the water taken from Boston's Quabbia reservoir, for instance, never makes it through the city's crumbling pipes. In Cleveland, 49 of the 164 municipally maintained bridges were declared "intolerable" in a 1978 federal inspection. In fact, some were so dangerous that they had to be closed.[5] Not surprisingly, the deepest cutbacks in maintenance have occurred in cities where the financial squeeze has been the most severe. A HUD-sponsored study by the Urban Institute, for example, showed that between 1973 and 1979 the city of Buffalo reduced its maintenance force by 42%; Philadelphia laid off 22%, and Newark 21%.[6]

The amount of money necessary to bring the quality of the infrastructure up to an acceptable level in declining cities may be astronomical. Just to repair Newark's streets, according to the Urban Institute study, could cost $200 million—or $600 for each resident. In Cleveland, where the bridge maintenance staff has been halved since 1972, the bill to repair the city's bridges was estimated at $150 million, or $240 per person.[7] In Chicago, where sewer backups are a part of daily life, the city believes that it could put half a billion dollars into the system and still see very little improvement.[8]

The policy of deferred maintenance is due partly to the realities of local politics. A year is a long time to the urban voter, and he reacts much more strongly to the prospect of an immediate cut in garbage collection than to the prospect of more potholes in the years to come. It is simply a political fact of life, as former HUD Assistant Secretary Robert Embry pointed out, that "poor people can't see the direct benefits of repairing a city's sewer lines." [9]

There is another reason for the acceptance of deterioration, however. The federal government will help to build municipal infrastructure, and sometimes fund the complete replacement of worn-out facilities, but it will rarely provide any money to keep new bridges and roads in good condition. It is very common to find a new multimillion-dollar expressway cutting through a system in which the rest of the road system is crumbling for want of routine repair.

The effect of this policy, according to the Department of Commerce's own studies, is "often [to] encourage early capital replacement, possibly earlier than is really necessary and/or desirable."[10] In other words, cities are encouraged by the federal government to choose the easy option of allowing infrastructure to deteriorate, rather than find ways of financing orderly repairs. Letting valuable facilities become dilapidated and useless is rewarded with federal projects, while keeping them well maintained leads to financial headaches.

The disparate political and practical problems involved in balancing the books led many cities, such as New York, into the ruinous practice of borrowing for current service expenditure on the collateral of anticipated future revenue. In the case of New York, the growth of this form of funding was quite dramatic. In the eight years up to 1973, net borrowing accounted for an average of 8% of the city's annual revenue growth, compared with 55% from state and federal sources, and 37% from local income. During the period 1973-75, however, borrowing exploded to 70% of the new revenue. State and local funding plummeted to 8%, and local income slid to 22%. Between the beginning of fiscal 1973 and the end of fiscal 1975, the city's outstanding general purpose debt rose by over $3 billion to $12.5 billion.[11] By 1975, New York was deep in the financial crisis from which it has yet to emerge. Several other cities are locked into similar situations.

The recent history of big city finance indicates that although the plight of inner cities is very real, and many of the complaints voiced by cities are valid, city officials have generally become obsessed with meeting short-term commitments with the minimum of political pain, irrespective of the future costs. The financial manipulations of New York City in the mid-1970s were so intricate that they almost reached the status of art, and yet this same ingenuity seems to have been absent in the decade or so before that when something of lasting benefit might have been achieved. Labor demands had been bought off with outrageous pay and pension concessions, and welfare benefits for many categories of recipients had been allowed to reach absurd levels. Yet little was done to alter the basic system of finance to meet changed circumstances or to examine really innovative ways of supplying neighborhood services.

The more money that has flowed to New York and many other older cities, the more benefits appear to have accrued to the providers of services, with only marginal improvements in efficiency. Although the financial case of cities may be strong, their track record provides little evidence to suggest that pouring more federal and state money into them is the answer to the underlying problem.

Urban Renewal—Thinking Big

While most older cities are now preoccupied with the question of municipal finance, city governments have usually seen their principal task—other than providing services—as that of improving conditions within neighborhoods and encouraging the general development of the city. In particular, city governments have seen it as their duty, in concert with other levels of government, to bring about beneficial changes in the housing and other physical amenities of the city for the general good of the people, on the assumption that such changes will not take place without government involvement.

The idea of renewing the housing stock and facilities of older cities became central to government policy during the late 1950s and

1960s, in both America and Europe. In its simplest form, renewal has involved moving people out of an area with substandard housing and facilities, housing them elsewhere temporarily, and then providing permanent new housing for them. Unfortunately, the results of such projects have in many instances been little short of disastrous. Relocating the residents of a neighborhood, and bulldozing great holes in the housing stock of an area, breaks up the social as well as the physical fabric of an area. With little regard to the idea of "community," it has been believed that people can be shuffled around and that somehow things will have necessarily improved if they end up in housing facilities which architects have deemed superior to the ones they left.

Some public housing projects have wrongly assumed that placing large numbers of poor people together would be beneficial; these have been examples of the spectacular failures that can result when "community" is ignored. The Pruitt-Igoe project in St. Louis won distinction for itself among such catastrophes. Completed in 1956, the development comprised 43 high-rise residential buildings (near the business district) for some 10,000 poor people. The structures were widely praised at the time, and the great majority of the tenants expressed satisfaction with their apartments. Yet within a few years, the entire development had become an urban jungle of violence and vandalism. By 1969, 40% of maintenance time and 30% of materials were devoted entirely to repairs resulting from vandalism. In that year alone, the project consumed 16,000 window shades, 20,000 panes of glass, and the services of an 84-man maintenance crew. The cost was half a million dollars.[12] Conditions became so increasingly bad that, by 1972, demolition of the entire development began.

We do appear to have learned something from these great planning disasters. We have moved away from strategies based exclusively on major rehousing projects to a more integrated view of city development, where consideration is given not only to housing, but also to the provision of jobs, transport facilities, education, and the other crucial elements of city life. One of the leading planners embodying this more sophisticated approach is James Rouse. Although his first successful projects consisted of standardized shopping centers, Rouse is now seen as a giant among city developers. In the 1960s he was responsible for the creation of Columbia, Maryland, said to be one of the most successful new towns in America. More recently, he has attracted wide acclaim for the festival marketplaces in central Boston and at Harborplace in Baltimore—developments that have brought new life to once stagnant central-city neighborhoods.

According to Rouse, nothing can be done to revive a declining city without thinking on a grand scale. A plan has to capture the imagination of all concerned—residents, businessmen, bankers— or it will surely fail. But it must not only stir the blood; it must also be a "big human plan that sees the city as a system and embraces all its parts and pieces." Urban renewal projects failed, Rouse contends, because they resulted in stifling, dehumanizing ghettoes. The well-conceived modern city plan, in contrast, is not solely concerned with producing large quantities of new housing, but rather it "unites planning with the expectancy of development, schedules it, costs it, reconciles the conflicts, finds the reinforcements between the physical, the social and the economic." [13]

It is difficult not to be carried along with the enthusiasm. But there are problems. A giant urban plan is like a giant economic plan. Both are seductive, and both are optimistic about the ability of the planner to take into account all possible factors and make allowances for them. Yet while great plans can be successful at achieving specific, limited goals, they invariably do so by snuffing out the intricate, invisible process of adjustment that is the strength of free economies and vibrant neighborhoods. No matter how much careful analysis is put into the planning process, or how many variables are fed into the computer, it is impossible to replicate the myriad forces that comprise a city or an economy. "All big plans are inevitably mistakes," argues Jane Jacobs, because they are rigid in both time and scale; they "stifle all alternatives that don't fit into their vision." [14]

Mrs. Jacobs, who has terrorized planners for years with her writings, is critical of virtually everything James Rouse stands for. She sees cities and neighborhoods as places that grow organically on a foundation of subtle local relationships so complex that no planner can create them, even if he understands their nature. Progress and improvement are possible, she contends, only after establishing a climate in which small, local developments can flourish—but great plans seem only to frustrate this process or literally bulldoze it out of existence.

It is interesting to note that the "successful" big plans are

32

almost always new plans. Perhaps it would be wise to wait a few years after the champagne corks have popped before we bestow great honors on this new generation of planners. The words of Jane Jacobs, written twenty years ago, should be remembered whenever a new project is opened. All too often, she wrote, viable, albeit distressed, communities are obliterated with the best of intentions and the most thorough planning, to make way for

> Low income projects that become worse centers of deliquency, vandalism and general social hopelessness than the slums they were supposed to replace. Middle income housing projects which are truly marvels of dullness and regimentation....Cultural centers that are unable to support a good bookstore. Civic centers that are avoided by everyone but bums, who have fewer choices of a loitering place than others. Commercial centers that are lackluster imitations of standardized suburban chainstore shopping. Promenades that go from no place to where and have no promenaders. Expressways that eviscerate great cities. This is not the rebuilding of cities, it is the sacking of cities.[15]

Perhaps the modern-day grand planners have learned how to avoid such results, but we should wait a little while before we join the celebrations—until we can assume the full consequences of the major surgery that has been carried out in many of our cities. While the verdict on the new wave of central-city developments must be many years away, there are some worrying signs that should not be ignored. In Pittsburgh the "Renaissance" project has run into bitter opposition from small shopkeepers who are being displaced through the power of eminent domain.[16] In many other cities, similar opposition has been voiced by neighborhoods torn apart in the drive to build convention centers and other business and tourist facilities that are in vogue.

Even in Boston, often seen as an example of what can be done with thoughtful planning, changes are taking place that should be a cause for concern. Undoubtedly the city *is* booming by any conventional measure. Construction goes ahead at a feverish pace, as high-rise offices, hotels, and residential buildings transform the central city. Ugly warehouses have been demolished, and the waterfront area is now a picturesque tourist attraction. Yet many argue that the city administration is so obsessed with downtown development that it is accelerating the demise of the city as a whole.

"It's almost as though the…administration were burning the city to save it," claims Boston novelist George V. Higgins.[17]

There are several reasons for such a reaction to the downtown boom. Many of the new buildings contribute little if anything to city revenues, thanks to generous tax concessions offered as bait to companies. This, in turn, has led to crushing property taxes for the rest of the city—taxes which have contributed to Boston's becoming an even more expensive place to live in than New York. This high cost of living has increased the exodus of hard-pressed residents out of the city's once vibrant ethnic districts.

These inner city working class communities, such as the Italian North End and the Irish neighborhoods of South Boston, have been the underlying strength of the city. But now they are being eroded both by physical redevelopment and by rising property values. The young, affluent professionals who shop in the fashionable boutiques of the restored Quincy Street Market are slowly displacing the traditional residents of the nearby North End. If the trend continues, says Councilman Lawrence DiCara, "it won't be long before the only people left in this city are the well-to-do professionals who work in all these new buildings and the very poor who have nowhere else to go." [18]

Councilman DiCara's worry points to the danger implicit in much of the most recent city redevelopment. The urban renewal projects of the 1960s were often disasters because they were based on the assumption that segregating and concentrating poor people in huge new housing developments was the same as rebuilding communities. More recent projects, however, have sought to bring middle- and upper-income residents and tourists into the centers of the cities as a means of strengthening the income and commercial base. Perhaps these developments correctly perceive the way in which cities will naturally evolve. On the other hand, they may result in failures even greater than those of urban renewal. We may see cities becoming hopelessly divided into three distinct segments: an expensive central core, based on retailing, office blocks, and tourism, where affluent residents are well protected and cut off from the seediness that surrounds the core; sprawling suburbs of white-collar workers who flow into the core on expressways and rail lines every morning and desert it every evening; and blighted inner neighborhoods populated by poor people who have no place in either the core or the suburbs, and where jobs shrink in number but

34

resentment and hopelessness grow. Failure to revive these inner neighborhoods, and to link them with the core, could undermine the most imaginative downtown plan.

Federal Housing Policy

For half a century, the federal government has been attempting to improve the supply and quality of housing as a means of improving urban and other neighborhoods. It now subsidizes the housing of over 3 million lower-income households and has insured or guaranteed homes purchased by another 7.9 million.[19] Since 1950, the federal government has subsidized the construction of 2.4 million apartments and 500,000 homes for lower-income families. Another 130,000 existing apartments and houses have also been subsidized.[20] The basic housing laws of the country are now so involved that they fill over 1,300 pages.[21]

Despite the general improvement of public- and private-sector housing, there are considerable problems with many government programs. The cost of public housing for low income families, for instance, now runs at only a little below the median price of all new housing, despite the planned lower quality of public units. There are a number of reasons for this. One important factor has been the Davis-Bacon Act.[22] The measure was passed in 1931 as a protection to local construction firms. It required that in all federal construction projects, including subsidized housing, workers on the site must be paid the "prevailing scale" for construction workers in the area. The determination of the prevailing scale is made by the U.S. Department of Labor, and normally it has been the case that the union rate is the benchmark. The Act has the effect of increasing labor costs of federal construction, and makes the use of lower-skilled workers less attractive.

The effect of the Davis-Bacon Act on federal construction cost has been substantial, according to some studies. A 1971 U.S. General Accounting Office study of 28 projects, for example, concluded that costs had been increased by 10% because of the improper administration of the Act, including the setting of artificially high "prevailing" rates.[23]

The cost of public housing has also been inflated by the general practice of placing projects on expensively cleared land rather than

35

on vacant land at the edge of cities. According to one estimate, units built on cleared slum sites have cost over 50% more than similar units on vacant sites.[24] It must be remembered, however, that normally there is strong local opposition to any suggestion that large public housing projects should be constructed anywhere but in low income neighborhoods.

The use of tax-exempt bonds as the principal form of financing has been another factor in the high cost of public housing. Although these bonds generally require a lower rate of interest (since it is tax free) than the prevailing rate in the market, there is a cost to the government associated with the marginal income tax rate that would be paid by the investor on other types of interest. According to a 1973 estimate by the National Housing Policy Review, the tax exemption costs the federal government almost as much as the total direct federal and local expenditures on public housing. This suggests that substantial savings might be made if other forms of finance were used.

The cumulative effect of these cost increments on the total subsidy given to families in public housing is substantial. The most detailed estimates conclude that new units cost approximately 25% more than comparable private units—with Davis-Bacon and the method of financing being the principal cause.[25] According to John Weicher, director of the Housing Markets Program of the Urban Institute and a former senior official at HUD, the combined capital and operating subsidy now runs at only slightly under $500 per month for each family housed. As Weicher points out:

> If that amount were provided directly to public housing tenants, it would enable them to rent almost any new apartment now being built privately. The subsidy by itself is nearly as much as the most recent poverty-level income ($6,662 for a family of four in 1978).... If the subsidy were given in cash directly to tenants, it would be enough to lift virtually all of them out of poverty.[26]

Subsidies of this level are possible, explains Weicher, because they go only to a small fraction of the eligible population:

> One of the most serious criticisms of public housing has been that it is fundamentally inequitable; a large benefit goes to a few households while nothing goes to a very large number that are similarly situated....Roughly speaking one [poor] family in twenty (in 1972) was being subsidized.[27]

36

It should not be assumed, however, that if public housing were more widely available it necessarily would lead to a more equitable subsidy. Britain provides a salutary example of how inefficient subsidies can be locked into a very widespread public housing program. About 40% of the entire population of Britain lives in "council housing" (i.e., public housing). In 1976, the average rent paid for a new three-bedroom council house was $65 per month, and the cumulative subsidy to taxpayers represented 8% of all public expenditures. Yet almost two-thirds of all council house tenants are from the skilled or managerial classes, and the average income of tenants is only a little below that of homeowners.[28]

The British experience suggests that once the number of people receiving a major subsidy reaches a politically significant proportion, it becomes extremely difficult to retain any justice or efficiency in the pattern of distribution. The recipients of the subsidy defend it with a determination that is rarely found among those who provide it.

Inefficiency and inequity have not been the only problems associated with the use of public housing in the United States as an instrument to improve urban conditions. Public housing projects have had a long history of social problems. Many things have contributed to the high rates of vandalism and serious crime. The very scale of some projects has perhaps doomed them. In some other cases poor management has led to difficulties. Tenant organizations have sometimes been used as an alternatives to professional managers, but lack of management skills has often reduced the effectiveness of that approach. High rise projects have been very troublesome, and large concentrations of public housing generally have many more problems than smaller numbers of units spread throughout a neighborhood.

One particularly interesting aspect of the social problems connected with public housing projects is that the success of a project does not appear to be closely correlated with the characteristics of the tenants. A study by the Urban Institute, for instance, found that although projects with social problems do tend to have more households on welfare than other projects, the characteristics of the project (including the condition of the neighborhood) are more significant than factors such as the size of the household, the proportion of unemployed residents, or the level of education.[29] Weicher notes that research of this kind is significant in itself.

The fact that the issue is raised at all is an ironic commentary on the change in perception about public housing. When the program was established in the 1930s, improved housing was expected to ameliorate social problems. Now program officials, tenants, and some analysts are willing to believe that social problems are affecting housing conditions, and for the worse, instead of the other way around.[30]

It is not just the public housing program for very low-income people that has been somewhat less than a roaring success at bringing about social improvement in the cities at a reasonable cost. Various other programs aimed at families with slightly higher incomes have also had their difficulties.

There is a wide range of programs for families with incomes a little higher than would normally be found among public housing tenants, but the most important in recent times have been two enacted in the late 1960s as modifications of earlier programs: Section 236, which provided mortgage subsidies to nonprofit and limited-dividend companies constructing moderate and low-rent apartments, together with a rent subsidy to tenants; and Section 235, which assisted low-income home buyers through a system of mortgage insurance involving no down payment.

By 1973 scandals had surfaced in both of these programs. Abandonment became common under Section 235. Sometimes this was because the housing was substandard and the buyer was unwilling to make repairs. Since no deposit was necessary, abandonment was often more economical than making repairs because the rate at which equity built up was very small. The low rate at which equity developed with such housing also encouraged owners to abandon their homes—if they wished to move within the first year or so—rather than pay the costs associated with a sale. Default rates were much greater than had been anticipated, leading to an increase in total costs. Rising operating costs also led to many defaults in the Section 236 program, and to an increased burden on low-income tenants required to pay a cost-related "basic rent."

Before 1960 housing acquired by the federal government through default or abandonment normally could be sold with few difficulties. But the accelerating rate of abandonment and default in the 1960s resulted in supply quickly outstripping demand. The total inventory of unsold houses held by the government was 27,000 in 1960. By 1972 it had reached 149,000. The number of apartments in government hands rose over the same period from 4,000 to 54,000.[31] In cities such as Detroit, large numbers of houses had been subsidized under the programs, and heavy abandonment occurred in some neighborhoods, leading to increased vandalism and other problems. This caused even more rapid abandonment.

In an effort to meet what was becoming a crisis, President Nixon set up a task force, the National Housing Policy Review, the recommendations of which became the foundation of the 1974 Housing and Community Development Act. The Act represented an important shift in policy regarding rental housing, away from direct subsidies for the construction of private units for low income tenants in favor of an approach which sought to provide tenants with money to pay for housing in the open market by means of a greater emphasis on rent subsidies.

It was felt that subsidizing people made a good deal more sense than subsidizing houses, and that the purely private market would provide the necessary housing much more efficiently. In addition, it was believed that supporting tenants directly would mean that there would be less of a tendency for these tenants to concentrate in district sections of neighborhoods, leading to social problems. Armed with his rent subsidy, the tenant would be able to shop around in the market. Mobility would be enhanced, and lower income families would be better integrated much more into the neighborhood.

This new policy took legislative form as Section 8 of the 1974 Act. Families were eligible if they had incomes of up to 80% of the local median—considerably higher than the usual limit for public housing. The subsidy was the payment of the difference between the "fair market rent" (FMR) for an apartment or house of a standard quality in the area, and 25% of the family's income. The FMR was related to family size, and a cost incentive to seek housing below the FMR was built into the subsidy. Thus, the tenant was guaranteed that there would be a ceiling on the proportion of his income going in rent, the landlord was guaranteed the FMR, and there was an upper limit on the government subsidy to each family. Developers could approach the local federal officials with plans for a new development to ensure that it met the Section 8 standards, and the federal government could invite private companies to construct projects. Landlords of existing units could have their buildings assessed, make improvements as necessary, and house Section 8 tenants.

39

The new construction Section 8 housing is, in a sense, a subsidy to place, since housing in specific locations is constructed because of the subsidy to the tenant. But even this part of the program is more loosely linked to place than most other federal programs. In the case of existing housing under Section 8, however, the tenant is free to choose his housing, providing it meets the quality standard and is no higher in cost than the FMR ceiling.

Like so many programs before it, Section 8 in practice has differed somewhat from Section 8 in theory. The program has certainly brought forth a large supply of housing. By 1977, 165,000 Section 8 units had been constructed and new apartments are now coming on line at the rate of about 100,000 a year. Over half a million households were receiving assistance by 1980, and an additional 120,000 were projected for 1981. The cost of the program, however, has been rising spectacularly. Under Section 8, HUD guarantees landlords that it will subsidize the rent paid by the tenant for the next twenty to forty years, and so an enormous commitment is built up. Between 1974 and 1979 alone, according to one writer, the government committed itself to an outlay of $130 billion through the program.[32] Senator William Armstrong has gone so far as to condemn the entire Section 8 program as "a potential bonanza for grasping politicians, influence peddlers and other rip-off artists.... Before it is through, this one provision may cost taxpayers upwards of $600 billion. It is sheer madness." [33]

Although estimates vary widely concerning the total commitment involved under Section 8, the criticism of the program does follow a pattern. In the first place, the fair-market-rent base for the subsidy is open to abuse, and it does not encourage developers to reduce construction costs. In fact, the FMR may be of only academic significance in many instances. An investigation by *Reader's Digest,* for example, found that although some Section 8 projects are very economical, and the subsidy is kept within reasonable bounds, others are the recipients of almost unbelievable amounts of federal money:

A classic example of this is New York City's luxurious Taino Towers. Located in East Harlem, Taino's 35 story concrete-and-glass towers contain 656 air-conditioned apartments, ranging from studios to duplexes and featuring double-sized windows and screened-in balconies. There are also greenhouses, an Olympic-sized swimming pool, an auditorium and a gymnasium. Apartments in this classy complex do not come cheap. A two-bedroom unit, for example, rents for $598. But *none* of the tenants will pay the fair market price. In fact, each apartment will be subsidized by the government to the tune of $9,608 a year—Section 8 covers $5,869 of this, the rest comes under an older HUD program. The total cost to the taxpayer for this one apartment complex: $6,302,848 each year.[34]

Such examples must be held in perspective, of course. They are not typical, and may be a better indication of the poor quality of HUD management than unsoundness in the Section 8 approach. The average monthly subsidy paid under the program for existing housing was only a little over $100 in 1976, which compared very favorably with other programs.[35] The cost is rising rapidly, however. Congressional Budget Office estimates for fiscal 1981 put the average monthly subsidy at between $250 and $300, depending on the rate of inflation.[36] The cost of subsidizing the rent of new Section 8 apartments is particularly high—about double the level for existing housing—even though it generally applies to households with slightly higher incomes. The fiscal 1981 budget estimates the monthly cost at $450 per unit, 50% more than the average monthly rental of new apartments in 1979, according to a Census Bureau study.[37] It should also be remembered that a higher proportion of new Section 8 units are efficiencies or one-bedroom units. This is not usually the case among new apartments, so the disparity is probably even wider.[38] Although precise calculations are difficult, and depend on many crucial assumptions, the evidence indicates that new Section 8 housing has not achieved any really significant cost savings over public housing, whatever social benefits have been achieved.

The second principal criticism levied against Section 8 has been its definition of a low-income family, that is, one which receives less than 80% of the median income of the area. Thus, in Washington, D.C., a family of four with an annual income of $16,000 is deemed poor enough to qualify for Section 8 assistance. Although this may indeed be a rather generous definition of poverty, it should be remembered that each family must contribute 25% of its income in rent before the subsidy is forthcoming, and that the FMR is a ceiling, and so the subsidy *does* decline as income rises. Therefore, the subsidy is often quite small. Furthermore, the work disincentive effect of a tight income requirement must be considered. The total loss of a rent subsidy when a higher-paid job is taken has the same disincentive effect as a heavy income tax.

The income characteristics of Section 8 tenants do not support the argument that aid is going to the well-off. In 1977 the median family income for households in new Section 8 housing was approximately $4,300, and in the case of existing units was about 20% lower—roughly the same as for families in public housing.[39] The comparison is not quite favorable, it must be admitted, when one notes that a large number of such "families" consist of a single, usually elderly, person. On the other hand, the program was always seen as a means of housing people with higher incomes than those of tenants in public housing.

The third principal criticism of Section 8, other than failings of management, is that the FMR tends to be higher than the true market rent in an area, leading to an inflated subsidy. Weicher estimates that this is probably true in at least half of the units in any metropolitan area. He points out that local governments receive an administrative fee based on the FMR, and so have every financial reason to gain from a high assessment of the FMR. The tenant also receives a credit if his actual rent is below the FMR, so he, too, will have no cause for complaint if it is set artificially high.

If one picks a careful path through the controversy surrounding the Section 8 program, the conclusion would seem to be that although the new housing element seems to be guilty of the mismanagement and waste connected with most federal housing programs, the existing housing element may be a step in the right direction. The subsidy necessary to house these Section 8 families runs at about half that required for public housing, although the families have comparable incomes. It has also been possible, by giving support to tenants instead of developers, to avoid many of the social problems associated with large concentrations of public housing. And it has encouraged the rehabilitation of the existing housing stock in poor neighborhoods, rather than following the more usual course in recent years of knocking down basically sound old buildings in order to replace them with expensive new dwellings.

Despite its problems, the existing housing program of Section 8 does appear to provide a good basis for a general approach aimed at improving the housing stock in depressed inner-city neighborhoods. A possible modification that might be considered as an improvement is some form of housing voucher, that is, a fixed subsidy unrelated to the rent of the housing actually chosen. This has the effect of simply boosting the income of the tenant, and allowing the housing market to function normally without the need for artificial FMRs. This may or may not be the answer to the shortcomings of the Section 8 program as it is now structured, but there is every indication that the effective way to revitalize inner city housing is not to tear down buildings and replace them at the taxpayers' expense, but to encourage rehabilitation through direct support to the tenant.

Although now we may be moving in the right direction, federal housing policies do not have a track record that is cause for pride. As John Weicher has observed:

> We continue to provide help to the poor by building new apartments for them, at great expense, even though most of them already live in adequate housing or housing that can easily and cheaply be brought up to standard. And we have so far found that many of our efforts to devise programs to help people buy homes end up by subsidizing those who would probably have bought in any case, or else are successful at a high price - in scandal and corruption as well as money.[40]

It does indeed seem to have been an implicit assumption of most federal housing policies that the only way to improve a neighborhood is to rebuild—with little regard to what is built or how much it costs. It is this philosophy that gave us Pruitt-Igoe and the staggering subsidies that have occurred under various programs. It has given us vast, ugly, depressing, and crime-ridden high-rise buildings, and it has given us high taxes. But it has not given us improved inner-city neighborhoods.

Local Housing Policies

Rent Control

Although many federal housing policies may be attacked as wasteful, they do at least *try* to improve housing conditions in poor inner-city neighborhoods. The great irony surrounding the housing problem in blighted areas, however, is that while the federal government is pouring money into these districts in an effort to improve the housing stock, the cities themselves are often pursuing policies that have the effect of aggravating the very problems that the federal government is trying to alleviate.

The clearest and most damaging example of such a counter-productive local policy is rent control. Swedish economist Assar Lindbeck once called rent control "the most efficient technique known to destroy a city—except for bombing." If one compares the South Bronx with Berlin, Hamburg, or even Hiroshima today, one might conclude he was actually understating the case. Arguably, rent control has been the most destructive housing policy ever adopted by cities.

Like all forms of price control, controls on rent are an attempt to hold the cost of an item below the price that would result from free interplay of supply and demand. The goal of the policy is to keep the cost of rental housing within the means of low-income families. Unfortunately for all concerned, the effect of the policy is to undermine the very foundations of the rental housing market, leading to shortages and a deteriorating housing stock.

Even if we could in some way "repeal" the laws of supply and demand, rent control would still be a highly questionable policy. When rent control is in force, tenants have the benefit of artificially low rents. Landlords, on the other hand, are faced with rising maintenance, fuel and other costs, and yet are denied the opportunity to earn the same market return that exists for other investments. The result is a net transfer of income from the landlord to the tenant. Now it is generally accepted that it is a reasonable goal of public policy to transfer some income from richer people to poorer people, but rent control does not do this. It merely transfers income from one segment of the population who happen to own property to another segment who happen to live in it. Transfers through the tax system are at least reasonably equitable, but to supplement this by requiring the providers of one commodity to subsidize their customers makes little sense.

Notwithstanding the whole issue of equity, rent control simply led to a decline in the quantity and quality of housing for the very group of people it is supposed to help. About one hundred cities in America, including New York and many other large declining cities, have some form of rent control. There is an enormous pressure of demand for rental housing, and yet the vacancy rate for such accommodation has been on the decline since 1974. By 1979 it had dropped to 4.8%, the lowest rate since the Census Bureau started keeping records twenty-five years ago. Anything below a 5% rate is considered dangerously low.[41]

Despite the pressure of demand, the units lost by conversion and abandonment are not being replaced at a sufficient rate to maintain total supply, which is contracting at approximately 1.5% each year. The rate of construction of rental units has been falling rapidly, and is now at its lowest level for two decades. Were it not for the government-subsidized sector, the situation would be even worse. Of multifamily units for rent, for instance, 75% of starts in 1979 were financed through government programs—up from 22% in 1972 and 44% in 1978. Despite this growth in the government's share, the number of units it provided actually fell.[42]

Rent control is not by any means the sole cause of this significant decline in the quantity of rental accommodation across the United States. To an extent, it reflects the population movements that are taking place. As the proportion of low-income families rises among the inner-city population, there is a dampening effect on the economics of renting. On average, rents rose from 20% of income in 1970 to 24% in 1976, and many of the poorest families are paying more than 35% of income in rent. Yet landlords have generally gained little from this. Between 1970 and 1978 rents rose by an average of 50%. Yet general prices increased by 70%, and many of the costs associated with property rose even more rapidly. Real estate taxes climbed 75%, for instance. Building costs rose 100%, and heating oil soared 156%.[43]

The economics of building or converting for sale, on the other hand, has become much more attractive. The tax code allows home buyers to deduct mortgage and property taxes from their income for tax purposes. This is a powerful incentive for middle-income renters to purchase instead, especially when inflation is pushing people into higher tax brackets and holds out the prospect of a substantial capital gain on property. Not surprisingly, the incentive for a landlord to convert lower-income rental units into condominiums is very powerful, leading to a contraction in the amount of existing low-cost rental property.

The increasing tendency of middle-income families to buy rather than rent has another important effect. Traditionally, there has been a "filtering down" process in the rental market. As buildings aged and neighborhoods changed, older, once middle-income rental units became available for poorer people. But the present state of affairs could better be described as "filtering up." Fewer private middle-income apartment buildings are being constructed, and yet a large number of low-income units are being converted for purchase by middle-income families.

Rent control has accelerated this trend. Controls have turned a bad situation for the landlord into a desperate one, leading to more conversion and abandonment. Even the possibility of rent control, writes George Sternlieb of Rutgers University Urban Policy Research Center, "has had a very strong chastening influence upon lender and builder willingness to become involved in the multi-family rental housing industry except under the most favorable circumstances." [44]

Rent control necessarily works against the long-term interests of the people it is designed to help. Shortages develop because artificially low rents lead to an increase in demand combined with a reduction in supply. In Washington, D.C., for example, eight years of rent control has produced a 12% reduction in available apartments. And in New York City, with its complicated system of rent "control" and rent "stabilization," the vacancy rate is now less than 3%.

When a controls-induced shortage develops, landlords are able to pick and choose their tenants. They will pick people with a steady job rather than those on welfare, professionals rather than transients, stable families rather than those headed by the mother. They can also practice the kind of racial and other discrimination that would be more difficult in a competitive, properly functioning market. Inequity is the by-product of controls, and it is the middle- and upper-income tenant who normally comes out on top. Rent control was quite beneficial for Mayor Edward Koch of New York, for instance, who in 1979 was paying $250 for a controlled apartment with a market rent closer to $400; and as it was for the president of the American Stock Exchange, who enjoyed an apartment valued at between $850 and $1,200 for a rent of just $660. [45]

Rent control also leads to declining maintenance levels. This is due partly to the simple fact that in a tight market, a shoddy product will sell because demand is high. But more often maintenance levels fall because the lid on the rent that can be charged means that the landlord makes savings wherever he can in order to turn at least some profit. We see this pattern of controls followed by a decline in housing quality in virtually every case of rent control.

46

Some "new-style" rent controls try to avoid this by allowing cost increases and repairs to be passed through to the tenant in the form of additions to the controlled rent. Often this is combined with a provision that the unit will no longer be controlled once it becomes vacant. But even in these cases the legal complexities involved often blunt the intended effect. The *Wall Street Journal* reported in a 1980 study of Los Angeles, where such a flexible system was introduced in 1979 to replace a 1978 rent freeze:

> Landlords are trying to improve their finances by cutting maintenance expenses. As a result, tenants often find themselves living in shabbier apartments. "We're doing nothing for renters now," says a manager who supervises 1,500 units here. "We're better off if a good tenant gets disgusted and moves." Suppliers who sell carpets, furniture and other items to landlords report that their business is off 30% to 70% since 1978.[46]

In the older cities with a long history of rent control, the result has been little short of a housing disaster. New York City, for example, has been under rent control in some form since the World War II. In neighborhoods such as the South Bronx, these controls have helped to destroy any hope of an economic return on rental housing. This has led to a deterioration of the housing stock through lack of maintenance and, in the extreme, to landlords employing the services of an arsonist so that at least the insurance can be collected. More honest landlords simply abandon their property to the ravages of local vandals and disappear. In some areas the downward spiral is so powerful that crime and blight have caused all but the most destitute tenants to move. In these neighborhoods, it is doubtful whether the removal of rent control, in itself, would have any impact, since the market has become so depressed. But the continuation of control removes any prospect of recovery, and encourages nearby areas to slide into the same condition of decay and blight.

These consequences of rent control are by no means confined to the United States. Similar results occur in other countries with rent restrictions. In 1975 the Fraser Institute of Canada published a collection of essays by leading economists covering the effects of rent control in five countries (the United States, France, Britain, Sweden and Austria) over the previous half-century. One of the authors, British economist F. G. Pennance, summarized the other essays as follows:

47

Their common message is simple, but devastating in its criticism of policy. It is that in every country examined, the introduction and continuation of rent control [restriction] regulation has done much more harm than good in rental housing markets—let alone the economy at large—by perpetuating shortages, encouraging immobility, swamping consumer preference, fostering dilapidation of the housing stock and eroding production incentives, distorting land-use patterns and the allocation of scarce resources, and all in the name of distributive justice it has manifestly failed to achieve because at best it has been related only randomly to the needs and individual circumstances of households.[47]

Britain provides a good example of these general results. Enacted as a "short-term" measure during the World War I, rent control is now a national institution. These controls managed, between 1915 and 1975, to reduce the quantity of rental units from 7.1 million to less than 3 million, and to create an acute shortage of rental units in cities despite a marked decline in the population of the inner cities.[48] While maintenance and building costs have soared, rents have been held at below market levels, leading to widespread dilapidation. If one visits any one of Britain's older cities, one sees the results—basically sound housing becoming slowly uninhabitable.

An interesting feature of the rental property market in Britain is that the proportion of rental property owned by individuals rather than property companies has been steadily rising; between 1971 and 1975 alone the proportion rose from 67% to 75% in the case of the heavily controlled furnished rental market.[49] This is not, by any means, an indication that such rental units are very attractive to individual investors. It is simply that individual investors cannot escape from the market with the same ease as property companies, who have the resources and legal skill to find ways of breaking leases and disposing of property. The individual owner finds it more difficult to escape. He or she is often a retired person who bought a house many years ago, hoping to obtain a modest income from it in later life, but now finds that he is subsidizing tenants who may be more affluent than himself. It is not so different in American cities. In the Bronx, for example, many landlords are small businessmen who invested their life savings in just one property, which is now a millstone around their neck. The well-organized slum lords may still be there, but the large property companies are generally long gone.

The most remarkable thing about rent control, in many ways, is

48

that it continues—and is even spreading—despite the fact that it is condemned by almost everyone who has any knowledge of housing. American Nobel Prize-winning economist Milton Friedman, a conservative, fulminates against it, and Swedish Nobel Prize-winning economist Gunnar Myrdal, a liberal, calls it one of the worst examples of government planning. Congressional leaders across the political spectrum attack it. *The New York Times* denounces it, as does the *Washington Post*. Some of the harshest criticisms of all have come from the minorities and other groups who are supposed to be the beneficiaries. As the *Amsterdam News*, New York's leading black newspaper, summed up the plight of so many tenants, "We in minority areas are forced to live in rat-infested apartments that resemble bombed-out war areas [which are]...rapidly increasing, instead of decreasing...solely because of rent control." [50]

Yet it continues, principally because it is so politically seductive. Rent controls are generally instituted during some perceived or real crisis (such as a war), or during a period of rapid inflation. When prices are rising, the clamor for controls begins. There are fewer landlords than tenants, and hearts seldom bleed for the property owner—seen usually in the folklore as at least "grasping," if not downright "oppressive." So it is easy for legislators to bow to the pressure. The benefit (low rent) is clear and immediate, while the cost (steady dilapidation and shortages) develops slowly, and can usually be blamed on the landlords in any case. As the effects of the controls become more evident, the more difficult it becomes to resist the pressure to retain or even to strengthen them.

When politicians acquire the courage to undo rent control, the full danger of flirting with the policy becomes clearer. There is seldom a rush to build new rental property when controls are relaxed. Rental property involves a long-term commitment, and so investors must be thoroughly convinced that controls will not be reimposed before new units are likely to be built. Invariably this "failure" of investors to respond to decontrol is taken as proof by tenant groups that rent control is not the cause of shortages.

A consensus seems to have developed among opponents of rent controls that the only way to remove them is to do so gradually, exempting units as they become vacant and decontrolling category after category. Yet even this approach has its pitfalls. When a limited way out is offered, the landlord has every incentive to seize it. In the 1979 Los Angeles law, for instance, control lapses when an apartment becomes vacant. This has had two effects. The tenant has every incentive to stay where he is, since he is no longer protected if he moves. The rate at which apartments are vacated in Los Angeles has indeed fallen sharply. But more importantly, the exemption for vacated units leads inevitably to what one Los Angeles tenants' lawyer describes as "a horrible incentive to evict" in order to get free of controls.[51]

The experience of rent control around the world shows just how much damage can be inflicted on a country's rented housing stock by the adoption of short-sighted "quick-fix" solutions to housing problems. Some people have argued that rent control has been the single most important cause of urban decay in America. Although this may be an exaggeration, it is clear that it has been a significant factor in the decline of many inner-city neighborhoods, and that there can be little prospect of seeing much physical improvement in these areas until is is ended.

Yet ending rent control presents considerable problems. Local politicians find it difficult to speak out against controls, and so it is unlikely that the initiative will come from that quarter. Some people, such as San Diego Mayor Peter Wilson in his recommendations to the Reagan transition team, have argued that federal pressures should be applied, including the threat that housing grants and other funds will be withheld from any city that has rent control. After all, this argument goes, why should the federal taxpayer be asked to spend money helping a city that refuses to repeal policies that are aggravating its problems? This is a very blunt political instrument to use, but it may be the only one that can get local officials off the hook. And it *can* work—the federal government used the same form of pressure to ensure state compliance with the 55-mph speed limit.

There is an economic problem with decontrol, however, as well as a political one. If controls are removed and rents allowed to find their market level, lower-rent housing would emerge through conversion or new construction. But housing involves major commitments and it can take a long time before supply increases sufficiently to have a significant impact on the market. In the meantime, rents would rise well above their long-run levels, leading to dislocation and adverse results for the poor. As *Washington Post* columnist William Raspberry has correctly noted, the short-term effect of removing controls would mean that the rich would bid up the rent of the housing that was available, "The bid-up price would spur development, of course, and 15 or 20 years from now there might be a housing glut in Washington—small comfort for the family that is put on the sidewalk today." [52]

The continuation of rent control, of course, is putting many poor people onto the sidewalk—because of conversion—and condemning others to live in deteriorating housing. The only way we can break out of this dilemma is to realize that we get what we pay for. Only by increasing the return that can be made from rental property will we ever obtain more and better homes for poor people. If people cannot afford the rents that are necessary for the provision of acceptable housing, and yet we see it as a goal of public policy that poor people should be able to live in the city, then the best solution would seem to be to supplement their income to meet the true cost of housing. We might do this through a modified version of Section 8, or by means of a housing voucher. Or we might consolidate all the needs of the poor into a form of negative income tax or minimum income guarantee.

If such a support mechanism were phased in during the period that rent control was phased out, it might restore the market with the least burden on the taxpayer and without wild fluctuations in the level of rents. The cost of this form of support might be considerable, but at the moment, we are merely masking those costs by requiring landlords to carry them and by allowing the rental housing stock to disappear. And, of course, part of the cost would simply be the price we have to pay for the folly of rent control.

Zoning and Building Codes

While rent control is the most obvious and damaging example of counterproductive housing policies at the local level, zoning and building codes have added to the problems of poor neighborhoods. In each case, the policy has been put forward on the basis that it protects the local community, and yet in each case the net effect has often been to undermine the interests of the urban poor.

Building codes are minimum standards for materials and work procedures established at the local level with the expressed aim of ensuring that buildings will be safe for those constructing or living in them. It would be difficult to question such a lofty purpose if that were all they were actually designed to do.

Basic building codes probably do ensure that safe materials and practices are used, but they also prevent the use of other equally safe—but less expensive—materials and practices. The result is that the cost of housing in many neighborhoods is much higher than it should be. The main reason for this situation is that many building codes exist solely for the protection of the building industry rather than the consumer. This is not a state of affairs unique to construction. We have seen regulations in many fields, such as trucking, telecommunications, and air travel, that have been established, on the face of it, to "maintain standards" or to "protect the consumer," but which have only had the effect of raising costs to the customer and protecting the industry leaders from competition.

According to Walter Williams, an authority on the impact of regulation on minorities, building regulations have the same results as other industry-supported restrictions. In particular, maintains Dr. Williams, many local codes have imposed considerable barriers in the way of housing for low-income families by reducing the use of prefabricated components, off-site labor, mass-produced housing sections, and less specialized labor. All manner of materials and work methods are prevented by building codes, with the result that costs are increased. Supporters of the codes maintain that they are for safety reasons, but in practice, contends Dr. Williams, they are chiefly for the age-old purpose of producer self-interest.[53]

A number of studies have tried to assess the validity of these claims, and to put some figure on the costs associated with building codes. The 1978 HUD Task Force on Housing estimated that as many as 10,000 political jurisdictions had building codes, and concluded that, "This uncoordinated system of differing and increased regulation is slowing down the building process and making the adoption of current and new potentially cost-saving ideas more difficult and expensive."[54]

A 1980 HUD study provided some indication of just how much the cost of housing might be reduced through sensible refinements in building codes and certain other local regulations.[55] The study was a field demonstration to test the cost implications of permitting technical innovations and streamlining permit procedures in the case of single-family housing. Four sites were chosen. Two were inner-city locations—Hayward in California and Shreveport in

Louisiana. In the Shreveport demonstration, the savings achieved amounted to 21% of the cost of a comparable unit built within the usual regulations. In Hayward, a similar streamlining of codes led to a cost reduction of 33%. These remarkable results induced the mayor of Hayward to institute "one stop" processing in order to reduce costs for all construction, and Shreveport has undertaken a complete review of its procedures.

Although the study was clearly limited in the number of sites chosen and the kind of housing involved, the results are sufficiently dramatic to suggest that local codes and other building restrictions contribute a significant and unnecessary addition to the cost of housing. HUD announced its intention to widen the field study in 1981, in order to obtain a better range of data. But from the evidence so far it is not easy to dispute the study's conclusions that "major reductions in housing costs can occur when local government helps in the process."

In addition to the codes themselves, a developer must also face the costs associated with local building permits and other regulations—the HUD study dealt with a number of these in each city. Part of these costs are due to the paperwork and legal fees involved. In Los Angeles, in 1978, a developer could face the prospect of contacting thirty-six different offices, filing twelve different application forms, and producing eighty-seven supporting documents before permission to build would be granted.[56] Not only are there direct costs of this nature, but the delays that accompany such complicated application procedures can add up to significant increases in costs. A 1978 study by Stephen Seidel found that the final price of a building would be increased by between 1% and 2% for each month of delay. In 1970, according to the study, the average delay was five months; by 1975 it had risen to thirteen months.[57] By 1978 the *Wall Street Journal* was reporting that delays of two years were common.[58]

Refining the great mass of local building codes to maintain safety while stimulating cost-cutting innovation would be no easy task. Some have argued that rather than fight 10,000 separate battles it would make more sense to consolidate the local codes into one simpler and more sensible federal building code. But this has many drawbacks. In the first place, one would have to be something of an optimist to expect that a single national code would actually be less onerous and inefficient than the local versions. With the exception of recent efforts to deregulate certain industries (i.e., to reduce *federal* regulation imposed on the industries), the usual result of putting regulatory power into federal hands is anything *but* cost-reducing. The most useful role for the federal government would be to serve as a source of information, providing comparisons of the effects of codes on costs, so that the consumer can become better aware of just how much unnecessary "protection" actually costs him.

Zoning may have a particularly damaging effect on many inner-city neighborhoods, because it not only adds to costs, but it also requires land-use patterns that may be very costly in social and employment terms. Zoning has developed through the 20th century on the assumption that a local government must step in to restrict incompatible land use in order to protect the value of an individual's property. In the United States, this has taken the form of dividing up a municipality into districts, in each of which only certain types of use are permitted. This normally means segregated use, whereby specific forms of use—light industrial, commercial, single family residential, etc.—are restricted to particular districts.

The system of zoning that now exists in the United States has come under attack from several directions. It is very complicated; most ordinances provide for boards of review, special exceptions, and procedures for appeal—all adding to the complexity and cost. It has also made city planning more difficult. Indeed, in many cases, dealing with zoning is the principal activity of a city's planning department. And zoning has also served to slow down, or even freeze, beneficial change in a large number of neighborhoods.[59]

Zoning is so pervasive in American cities that it is almost taken for granted that without it, there would be chaos. But in one major city, at least, development appears to have occurred in a reasonably orderly fashion without it. Houston is the fifth largest city in the country. It has a population of 1.5 million, up 26% from 1970, and it has no zoning. Houston may not be everyone's idea of an architectural paradise, but there are few rapidly growing cities that do have that reputation. Yet despite the absence of zoning, it has managed to maintain order and flexibility during its growth.

It would not be correct to say that there are *no* land use controls in Houston. There are a number of citywide regulations which would, for example, prevent slaughterhouses being built next to churches, or other forms of incompatible uses; and the common law of nuisance which gives residents additional protection from polluting industries and similar activities. Restrictive covenants are also common. These are collective agreements entered into by purchasers of newly developed subdivisions of the city. They have the effect of controlling the use of properties within the unit for a specified period, unless there is agreement among the residents to permit an alteration or to extend the period. The sovereign body dealing with the use of land is thus the membership of the subdivision itself, not the city as a whole or its government. The general restrictions apply across the city, but these do not have the effect of reserving certain districts for particular uses.

The experience of zoning in Houston provides an illustration of how the real estate market leads to a quite rational use of land. More important, it gives an indication of how conventional zoning can undermine the stability of a neighborhood and hasten its decay.[60]

Bernard Siegan, in his account of Houston, has pointed out that the price mechanism operating in the land market leads to a pattern of use that tends to enhance property values rather than weaken them. Gas stations might be able to save in land costs by locating in quiet residential streets, but these areas do not provide the busy thoroughfare traffic that stations need, and so they do not locate there. In Houston there is a strong tendency for industrial users to concentrate and separate themselves from residential users—again the price of land and citywide restrictions encourage this. Commercial activity normally is found along major streets, without being required to conform to that pattern by zoning.[61] And there is every indication that the people of Houston are quite happy with this way of allocating land uses, since they have voted down various zoning proposals.

Perhaps the most interesting aspect of Houston's non-zoning is the manner in which sensible mixed use of land has developed. It is quite common to find home businesses and light commercial activities in many residential neighborhoods—of the kind that serve the residents. As Houston's planning director points out, this diversity is far more beneficial to poorer areas than the uniformity that is the hallmark of zoning:

> In older segments of the city...the land use pattern is predominantly single family, with low-to-moderate income housing placed rather closely together. While along major

55

thoroughfares there may be active non-residential commercial development, many quiet residential neighborhoods can be found which also contain small grocery stores, bars, laundries and other types of service businesses. These exist only because they are conveniently located to serve a population of general low mobility. Industrial areas may also be found close to older residential areas. While some of these industries may create some pollution within the adjacent residential areas, most do not have a deteriorating effect and, in fact, provide job opportunities for low-to-moderate income groups conveniently located near their homes.

The mixed land use pattern that is found in some sections of the city should, therefore, not be viewed as all bad. In a lower income area, the availability of car-repair services, eating establishments, bars, and such service outlets makes for an "attractive" neighborhood in the sense of convenience for a group that has low mobility. The ability to establish a business in one's garage or home contributes to easy entry of individuals into the economic system. Many a small business has been started in a home or garage.[62]

The mixed use land pattern described by Roscoe Jones is of central importance. Segregation of uses has been the principal theme of most zoning ordinances, and this has inhibited the kind of activity that is possible in Houston. Of course, Houston is a bustling, almost frontier city, and is very Texan, so the absence of zoning in other cities would not necessarily produce the same kind of architecture or types of industrial and commercial uses. The pattern in each city would reflect the interplay of local factors. But the mixed land use we see in Houston's low-income neighborhoods would seem to be an essential element in their stability and vitality. As we shall see later, Jane Jacobs and others argue that a mixture of activities and use of buildings is an essential precondition for a successful low-income area. This is not only for economic reasons, Jacobs argues, but more importantly because it enhances the feeling of safety in the neighborhood and so allows various activities to flourish.

While the most damaging consequences of restrictive zoning are on economic and social conditions, it should also be noted that zoning, like many building codes, has a tendency to push up the costs of housing and business. In the first place, any kind of restricted land use will reduce the efficiency of the land market. If a certain type of development is prevented by zoning, then a less attractive—that is, more costly—site must be chosen. In addition, minimum-lot-size requirements have the effect of reducing the profitability of low-income housing and many new business developments.

It is difficult to reach any precise conclusion regarding the total impact of zoning on the cost of buildings in a city. In more affluent neighborhoods, minimum lot sizes may lead to the same results as restrictive covenants or the unfettered market. But spokesmen for Houston do maintain that in general significant cost reductions have been achieved for many types of housing. They maintain, in particular, that the absence of zoning has helped to bring down the cost of constructing and operating apartment buildings as well as medium- and low-income housing. Construction innovations are used that are often impossible in zoned cities. "It is no accident," contends Roscoe Jones, "that Houston continues to be recognized for maintaining comparatively low-cost and high-quality housing of all types available in the housing market." [63]

The Government and Business in the Cities

Government policies that have influenced the state of business in urban areas fall into roughly two categories. There is a broad range of regulatory and tax policies which affect the complexity and cost of doing business in the city. And there is also a number of grant, loan, and training programs which aim to provide "front end" support aimed at encouraging the creation of jobs for less employable city residents. Many of these policies, of course, are not limited to the urban setting, let alone declining cities, but they are seen by many as an essential part of any program likely to revive depressed urban neighborhoods.

The Regulatory Nightmare

While business as a whole claims, quite justifiably, that federal regulation has been a major impediment to economic growth, the burden seems to have fallen particularly heavily on the small business sector, despite the fact that small companies are given an exemption from certain categories of regulation. The reason that the uneven load of regulation has been so damaging for cities is that there is considerable evidence that *small* firms are by far the most important in creating the quantity and type of jobs most suitable for inner-city neighborhoods. The small businesses tend to produce more jobs for younger, unskilled people, and they are virtually the only firms that are creating net, new jobs in many declining neighborhoods. The full evidence to support this is given in chapter 3.

Government regulation and paperwork, together with taxation and regulation, are cited continuously by small companies as the greatest problems they face. In the central cities, regulation seems to be particularly troublesome. A 1978 survey of businesses in ten sample cities, by the Joint Economic Committee of Congress, for instance, found that comments from the 1,300 businesses that responded to their questionnaire "overwhelmingly cited the need for reduced federal paperwork and regulation. This was the single most widely expressed sentiment and was universally stated by all types and sizes of firms in all cities." [64]

The 1980 White House Conference on Small Business voiced the same concern. "We are here to petition for less," said Arthur Levitt, chairman of the conference. "We're looking for *less* interference and *less* harassment." [65]

A principal reason for the strong concern expressed by the small sector is that regulations do not generally distinguish between companies by size. But while there is some equality in the volumes of regulations that are sent to companies, this does not mean that there is equality in their impact. The small firms usually lack the skilled employees necessary to interpret the regulations and fill in the forms. Furthermore, there are considerable economies of scale in form-filling. The total cost of completing the paperwork required by an agency may be approximately the same to a company with sales of $500 million as it is for a firm with sales of $500,000, but as a proportion of costs per unit, the small firm is hardly treated equally.

Murray Weidenbaum, chairman of President Reagan's Council of Economic Advisors, has provided many examples of the disproportionate costs of federal regulation. In the late 1960s the foundry industry began to lose small plants specializing in limited orders, primarily because the cost of mandated EPA emission control expenditures approached or even exceeded the net worth of their existing operations. Large firms, on the other hand, were able

58

to absorb the cost.[66] Weidenbaum found similar effects in most other industries.

The cost of such regulations and their associated paperwork can be very heavy, and the purely financial cost may be the least important for the small businessman. Surveys by the National Federation of Independent Business, and various other small business groups, indicate that the desire for independence is a major motivating force behind the creation of small firms by entrepreneurs. The professional manager in a large concern often has the bureaucratic approach to business that enables him to deal with the regulatory maze. But it is rare to find a small entrepreneur who goes into business because he likes filling in forms.

Fortunately, there are grounds for some optimism that the regulatory load on the small sector may be reduced to the benefit of both the entrepreneurs themselves and those who are employed by them. Pressure for deregulation has been growing; and already in industries such as telecommunications and trucking, rules have been simplified and the market has been opened up to new competition, a good deal of which has come from new, small companies. In addition, the 1980 Regulatory Flexibility Act established a two-tier approach to regulation. This accepted the fact that the same regulation may pose quite unequal burdens on different sizes of companies, and it required agencies to consider this when instituting new regulations. If necessary, the agency must modify the rule, or exempt small companies entirely, if unreasonable hardship results for such firms. The Reagan Administration is also committed to a policy of deregulation, and so further steps can be expected to reduce the obstacles facing small companies.

Of course the federal government represents only one level of the regulatory process. State and city laws are superimposed on everything that comes from Washington. In many cities these local regulations and permits are the last straw for the would-be businessman.

Cities have an unfortunate habit of assuming that economic health is synonymous with the health of the large corporate sector. Enormous amounts of time and money will be spent by a city to deal with the grievances of its major corporations, while thousands of tiny companies that employ far more people are overlooked. This is perhaps not all that surprising, according to *Fortune* magazine. In one of its surveys of New York City, the magazine noted that, "If the city succeeds in keeping Pan Am happy, it will bathe in the nice, warm approval of the New York Times....But when a city official manages somehow to improve the lot of a small manufacturer, nobody notices." [67]

This attention to the interests of a few large companies, rather than to the mass of small operations, is a key part of the problem of many older cities. It is the kind of attention that leads to very generous property tax abatement and other incentives to major corporations, which will have only a marginal effect in poor areas, which must then be paid for by increasing the burden on those who are in fact the ones who offer most hope.

Although the small business sector in New York may not carry much political weight, it is the backbone of the local economy. Of the 190,000 firms in the city, 98% employ fewer than a hundred workers, and 90% fewer than twenty. While much attention is given to retaining corporate headquarters in downtown Manhattan, it is the steady loss of these small companies that should be causing most concern. In the last decade, the city has lost well over half a million jobs, and yet less than 10% of these can be traced to the relocation of corporate headquarters.[68] It is manufacturing, and in particular small manufacturing, that has led the exodus.

Despite the crucial importance of the small busines sector for the economic health of New York and other cities, the tendency has been to soak these firms whenever a boost in revenues is needed. City taxes on business have been rising, supplemented by what *Fortune* has called the "nightmarish array of permit and inspection fees that multiplied geometrically both in number and price." These taxes and fees represent a significant disincentive compared with the cost of establishing elsewhere:

> Taken individually, the fees were a nuisance. But piled on top of one another, and on top of general taxes, they created a powerful incentive for many businessmen to find another place to operate. Moreover, in the 1960s, upstate counties and other states, variously offering lower taxes, cheaper labor, or space for expansion, began sending industrial recruiters to lure New York businessmen away from the city. By 1974, the South Bronx had lost 650 of the 2,000 manufacturers who had been there in 1959, and 17,600 of the 54,037 jobs they had provided. Few new businessmen moved in, and those who did, among them the Hunts Point wholesale food market and a Coca-Cola warehouse, brought most of their employees with them from elsewhere in the city.[69]

The cost and complexity of regulation at the local level contributes to what companies perceive as the attitude of the city to the business community, and this is an essential part of what they see as the business *climate* in the city. It is very clear, from the 1978 Joint Economic Committee survey, that the attitude of the city government is crucial to companies' plans for future development. The study found that the attitude of the city government was the most widely cited factor affecting the decision to stay and expand in the present location, followed closely by the crime level. On average, these factors were well above the market demand for the company's products, and well above tax rates or the availability of financing.[70]

The study also found a strong correlation between the feeling among businesses that the city had a favorable climate with plans by companies to increase their work force.[71] It is worth noting in this regard that Dallas headed the list with 98.6% of respondents in the city reporting that they had a favorable perception of the business climate. Detroit, on the other hand, received a 30.7% favorable rating, and New York was at the bottom of the list with 27.2%.[72]

The study concluded that its findings indicated that direct financial support for city businesses in depressed areas is unlikely to be successful unless cities upgrade their facilities and make a strong effort to cooperate with the business community:

> While the federal government can, and in the past has attempted to assist in many of these areas they remain essentially the domain of local governments. Local tax rate, and, most particularly, the city government attitude towards business are not only important, but also vary significantly between the most favorable and least favorable cities....Regardless of federal initiatives...if the city government attitude toward business and the quality of life are not perceived as positive, the effectiveness of discreet programs and policies is likely to be diminished.[73]

Many cities now appear to be taking these sentiments to heart, and seeking ways of reducing the red tape and costs that they impose on businesses. But it is not possible to deal with small entrepreneurs over a martini at City Hall, or to provide them with a custom-made package of tax abatement and other concessions. It is possible to reach them only through a general policy of deregulation and tax reduction aimed at creating a favorable entrepreneurial climate in which they might flourish.

A number of federal programs have provided direct financing in an effort to encourage economic development in poorer areas. The principal ones are the Community Development Block Grants (CDBG), the Urban Development Action Grants (UDAG), grants and loans through the Economic Development Administration (EDA), and various programs of the Small Business Administration (SBA).

The CDBG program, instituted in 1974, was a consolidation of ten categorical sources of assistance into one program, with much greater local discretion over the use of the money. The program aims to help development in distressed areas, and there are eligibility requirements based on housing conditions, poverty, and similar indicators of need. EDA was established in 1965 by the Public Works and Economic Development Act, "to help generate employment opportunities and improve levels of living in areas that have not shared our national prosperity." EDA provides loans and grants for public works, aimed at improving infrastructure, and a loan program for business development. As with CDBG, EDA money is available only if a locality meets certain criteria of economc distress.

The most interesting and innovative of the development-assistance programs is UDAG. The others, while very important to cities, are more conventional in their method and targeting approach. UDAG was unveiled by the Carter Administration in 1978, with a $400 million (now $675 million) budget, and was described by Mr. Carter as the "centerpiece" of his urban policy.

Although UDAG, like the other programs, can only be given to areas that comply with certain criteria of distress, it differs in that it is discretionary. Even more important, the purpose of UDAG is to use public funds as a means of levering private finance in order to make specific commercial projects possible in distressed areas. In theory at least, the program provides just enough public money to ensure that an otherwise private venture will go ahead. The city must demonstrate to the satisfaction of the federal government that were it not for the grant, the necessary private finance would desert the project. It provides a mechanism, in other words, for the city to provide "up-front" money as part of an agreement with the private sector. This private participation is a requirement for the grant, which may be used to provide infrastructure for the development, or as part of the project itself.

UDAG has a good image in the world of urban development, and this helped to save it from complete annihilation in the first barrage of budget cuts in 1981. The physical results of the program can also be seen in many cities. Supporters of UDAG point out that it represents a true partnership between the private and public sectors, for mutual benefit, in the tradition of urban economic development in America. They also argue that it is highly efficient. According to some evaluations, UDAG brings forth, or levers, between five and six dollars of private money for every dollar committed by the government.[74]

While UDAG, like Section 8 in the housing field, is a significant step forward in the quest for an appropriate set of solutions for the urban problem, it does appear to have some serious shortcomings. In the first place, UDAG, like all discretionary programs, is subject to the realities of politics. Many have described UDAG as little more than an "urban slush fund," and according to Business Week, the whole program was devised by the Carter Administration "after political sophisticates in the Administration and the Congress took a searching look at where Carter's votes had come from in 1976." [75] Certainly the awarding of UDAGs (during the primaries and the election of 1980) followed a pattern that did not exactly ignore the potential political benefits.

Although this aspect of the UDAG program may be dismissed as merely part of The American Way, it does lend credence to the claim of critics that UDAG is much less efficient than its supporters claim. Robert Poole, in his analysis of UDAG, for example, points to case after case, drawn from studies by the government's own General Accounting Office, that suggest that many of the projects for which UDAG money was said to be essential would have proceeded in any case.[76] If UDAG support is available only if a company can show that it cannot go ahead without it, no self-respecting company in America would be unable to produce the "proof." Obviously, it is impossible to know just how many UDAGs were the reward for corporate bluff or city politicians, but there is very good cause to be highly skeptical of the leverage claims.

Even when UDAG clearly makes the difference, it is not always clear that there is real benefit to the residents of distressed areas. Several UDAGs have been used to construct middle- and upper-income apartments in cities such as Baltimore and Chicago, and many of the new downtown Sheraton and Hyatt hotels received considerable assistance from UDAG. The effect of such projects on the residents of the poor neighborhoods of a city is, to say the least, indirect.

Some of the hotels, and similar projects supported by UDAGs, do, of course, provide employment for the young, unskilled labor force in the inner cities, but the number of jobs is likely to be quite limited. The whole UDAG approach is ill-suited to the small entrepreneur—the prime job generator. Companies taking part in a UDAG project must be willing to enter into the bureaucratic planning process. Not only are small, individualistic firms disinclined to do this, but the costs and risks of dealing with such companies, from the government's point of view, is very high. Nevertheless, it should not be overlooked that although a UDAG project may have a very limited *direct* impact on neighborhood employment, it may provide the nucleus for other activity. Smaller firms can become suppliers for larger UDAG businesses, or they may simply take advantage of the economic climate provided by the existence of the project. Even a hotel for affluent tourists generates prosperity and employment for people in the city who are unconnected with the hotel trade. Seen in this context, there may be a good argument for such publicly supported projects as a *catalyst* for development, even though the direct effect might be limited.

Some critics of UDAG and similar aid programs, however, point to deeper, conceptual problems with the approach. Robert Poole, for example, argues that the most successful economic development in poor areas, and in other countries, occurs within a *climate* of incentives, rather than through direct support. In such an environment of low taxes and regulation, investors are more willing to take risks. And these investors are not so much the "safe" ones that take part in government projects, but the smaller, more innovative people who bring about more rapid job and income generation. The federal grant approach, by design, targets assistance to the chosen few. The criteria for selection are at worst political and arbitrary, and at best the product of a general plan for the city. But, as Poole argues, such plans are invariably a straitjacket on the kind of innovative development that could really provide a boost to a declining city:

Rather than encouraging a climate of mobility and flexibility, the grant programs serve to increase the level of local and national bureaucracy, to add regulations which increase the time and cost of projects, and—to the extent that their accompanying "planning" succeeds—to ossify the local economy rather than encouraging its dynamism.[77]

The Small Business Administration, unlike UDAG, is aimed specifically at the small company. In addition, its Section 8(a) and other programs are designed to channel assistance to minority entrepreneurs. While SBA is not specifically an urban program, it is seen by many as a crucial part of urban redevelopment.

But it is unlikely that the SBA will ever be able to expand its quite marginal role in stimulating small inner-city firms. For one thing, the managment of SBA and the criteria of eligibility leave a great deal to be desired. The very definition of "small" at the SBA is interesting in itself. Until 1980, almost 99% of all business could qualify under SBA's rules. Admittedly, under new regulations the proportion was slashed to a mere 95%, but even so there are wide disparities in the eligibility criteria between different industries. These disparities are defended by the SBA on the grounds that a primary goal of the agency is to promote competition, and that it is necessary to adjust eligibility standards depending on the level of concentration in an industry. This does mean, however, that a firm making men's shoes, with 2,500 employees, would qualify, while a motorcycle dealer with sixteen would not.[78]

The eligibility criteria are so complex that many of the companies that qualify either do not realize it, or fail for various technical reasons to receive support, while others of more questionable need seem to obtain finance. The situation is particularly chaotic in the SBA's 8(a) program, aimed at the "economically disadvantaged." According to the *Washington Post,* "The federal government's flagship program to foster minority business is in many cases doing precisely the opposite of what was intended. It is helping rich white contractors get richer and turning away hundreds of the poor and disadvantaged it was designed to assist."[79]

In its 1979 audit, the SBA found that 21% of the firms receiving loans under the 8(a) minority program had been operated by unqualified people—many of them white businessmen using minorities as fronts. Several of the recipients were millionaires.[80]

Nearly $4 billion had been distributed under Section 8(a) during the previous thirteen years.

Assuming that the SBA were to decide that millionaires were not economically disadvantaged, and that the agency could come up with a definition of "small" that did not include almost every business in the country, there would still be enormous obstacles to its having much real impact on new, small companies. There is an inherent dilemma in the grant and loan approach as a means of helping small entrepreneurs. Since public money is being put at risk, it is only proper that safeguards should be applied. But these safeguards, no matter how rational, increase the complexity of the loan process. In addition, careful government bureaucrats, like careful bankers, take a conservative attitude to risk. The company with a good, proven record and solid financial base has a much better chance of securing a loan than the innovative, new, but unproven firm.

The problem with this policy is that while it does safeguard the public's money, it means also that money does not tend to find its way to firms that are most likely to create new jobs. An MIT study by David Birch highlights the inescapable shortcomings of the loan approach to encouraging new firms. Birch studied the job creating record of companies, using data from 5.6 million establishments across America—encompassing 80% of all private sector employment. From this data Birch concluded that the most effective job-creating firms had certain distinct characteristics:

> The job creating firm tends to be small. It tends to be dynamic, or unstable, depending on your viewpoint—the kind of firm that banks feel very uncomfortable about....In short, the firms that can and do generate the most jobs are the ones that are the most difficult to reach through conventional policy initiatives.
>
> ...It is no wonder that efforts to stem the tide of job decline have been so frustrating—and largely unsuccessful. The firms that such efforts must reach are the most difficult to reach and the most difficult to work with. They are small. They tend to be independent. They are volatile. The very spirit that gives them their volatility and job creating powers is the same spirit that makes them unpromising partners for the development administrator.[81]

Birch argues that the kind of entrepreneur who has the greatest potential as a creator of jobs is not the sort of person who fills out

66

forms or has an easy rapport with bureaucrats or bankers. A recent survey of its members by the National Federation of Independent Business demonstrated some of the consequences of Birch's findings. The survey found that only just over 3% of existing small companies had used any government finance at all in starting their firms, and in fewer than half of these cases was it the principal source of funding. In contrast, almost 60% of American small companies were started with capital provided primarily by the owner or his friends.[82]

The inescapable conclusion from findings such as these is that government-loan programs aimed at encouraging job creation are likely to remain inefficient, no matter how the administration of the programs is improved. If SBA and other government officials were even able to locate the potential small businessman, and persuade him to fill out the forms, the best job generators are so volatile that the wastage rate and bureaucratic time costs would be enormous. The alternative approach would be to reduce the unnecessary costs and red tape that frustrate innovative entrepreneurs and increase the amount of capital they require to start their businesses. Removing barriers to small, independent firms is far more likely to be successful than trying to find efficient ways to provide them with enough cash to overcome the barriers.

Inner-City Employment

If there has been one clear failure in urban policy since World War II, it has been the attempt to create lasting employment for poor inner-city residents. The unemployment rates among young, minority groups in the cities has been particularly high. The depressing situation has been resistant to government programs, and it has added racial tension to the economic plight of many neighborhoods.

Some analysts have argued that certain of the programs aimed at reducing unemployment in the central cities have not only been ineffective and wasteful, but have actually contributed to the already explosive situation. The minimum wage, in particular, has been attacked as a crude attempt to defy the natural operation of the labor market that has backfired against the very group it was designed to help. Just as rent control has reduced the supply of a product (rental housing) by keeping the price below the market rate, so minimum wage has reduced the demand for a service (labor) by keeping the price artificially high. Writers such as Walter Williams point out that minimum wage simply prices the least employable people out of the labor market—primarily those who are young, unskilled, and black. And there are plenty of these people in the inner city.

Williams marshals persuasive evidence to support his contention that minimum wage is a primary cause of high unemployment among young minorities. He points out that in 1948 black youth unemployment was roughly the same as the rate among white youth. Indeed, for 16-17-year-olds the rate was actually lower than among whites. By 1976, when the minimum wage was firmly entrenched, the unemployment rate among young blacks was running at over double the rate among young whites. Williams contends that it would be hard to maintain that the divergence must be due to an increase in racial discrimination over the period. The only possible reason for the change, he argues, is the effect of minimum wage. As the minimum wage edged further and further away from the economic wage rate, so the employment effect on young minorities became more severe.[83]

Evidence to support Dr. Williams's hypothesis is available from the experience of other countries. In France, for instance, the minimum wage covers virtually all workers (as opposed to about 85% in the United States). Between 1969 and 1979 the French minimum wage rose by 285%—compared with a rise in the consumer price index of 141%. The result of this, according to an analysis by André Fourcans, was quite dramatic: "During 1969-1979 the overall unemployment rate jumped from 2.3% to 6%....The rate for young men—15 to 24 years old—went from about 1% to a little over 10%; for young women in this same age bracket it increased from 1.5% to almost 18%." Professor Fourcans's econometric analysis of the rates, which took into account demographic and other factors, concluded that between 60% and 85% of the rise in the unemployment rate during the 1970s was due to minimum wage.[84]

Not everyone agrees that there is such a strong relationship between minimum wage and high levels of unemployment among young people in the cities. Some argue that discrimination is still the primary factor, and others point out that there has been a general exodus of jobs from the city. Others still maintain that the welfare system has provided a strong disincentive for people not to accept low-paid jobs, and that this is a more important cause of the rise in the unemployment rate among the least employable than the minimum wage.

The discrimination argument is difficult to accept. For it to be true there would need to have been a marked increase in prejudice in recent years. Given the changes in attitudes and the law that have taken place in the last twenty years one would have expected to see a decline in the unemployment rates of young minorities, not an increase.

It is true that there has been a decline in job opportunities in the cities. But in a functioning labor market the result of this would have been a fall in the price of labor, making the inner-city work force more attractive to certain employers. Minimum wage, by putting a floor on wage levels, prevents this adjustment from taking place, and ensures that the outflow of jobs continues. For those who are prepared to break the law, such as illegal alien workers and their employers, there remains a labor market, but those who are honest are frozen out of it.

There does seem to be a good deal of validity, however, in the argument that the welfare system does have an effect on unemployment rates, and that it weakens the sensitivity of the labor market to wage changes. In other words, runs the argument, the removal of minimum wage would not mean that there would be a dramatic increase in jobs—albeit low-paid jobs—in the cities because the welfare system makes it uneconomic for people to take jobs at low wage rates. It is not the *level* of welfare that produces this result, it is said, so much as the effective tax rates that a welfare recipient faces. He is in a poverty trap. If he accepts a job he loses certain welfare benefits, and this has the same impact on him as very high rates of marginal tax: Some recipients face effective tax rates of the level that are normally reserved for the highest income earners in the country.

There seems little doubt that this welfare effect is a contributor to unemployment among the least skilled, and that there should be reform to reduce the effective tax rate that the welfare recipient experiences when he takes a job. But it is not a sufficient explanation for the unemployment rate in the cities. Many young people desire work even though the immediate economic benefits are slight because they correctly see that the low-paid job is just the first rung on a ladder. Yet these people often can find no work in the city in the legal labor market. The effective tax rate may be a strong disincentive for older welfare recipients with heavy family commitments, but it is not a good explanation for the heavy unemployment among the many young city residents who are eager for virtually any job.

There are a number of government programs that have sought to help the situation by improving the employability of low-skilled people through job-training assistance, either in the public sector or by giving private employers grants to hire and train workers. Expenditures on these programs, both in total terms and as a proportion of the federal budget, have been rising steadily since the 1960s. The most important of these programs have been those emanating from the 1973 Comprehensive Employment and Training Act (CETA).

Although these programs may be responsible for some notable successes in some individual cases, it is doubtful whether the long-term employment effect of CETA has been more than marginal. There has not been any really noticeable impact on unemployment rates in the cities as a result of CETA. Its critics argue that it seems to result in either dead-end public sector jobs, or in the kind of training that does not particularly fit the worker for the employment, such as it is, that exists in the cities. The problem with CETA, it may be argued, is that it trains people for jobs that are no longer there because other policies have reduced the incentives for businesses to stay or start in the inner city.

Even some of those who were once strong supporters of the CETA program have become disillusioned with it. Representative Shirley Chisholm probably spoke for many of her liberal colleagues when she admitted recently:

> The reality remains, however, that years of federal efforts and billions of federal dollars have not brought forth prosperity and full employment to minority communities. "Cooling-off programs," as they are perceived in many poor neighborhoods, helped defuse hostility, but raised fake hopes of deliverance from the cycle of welfare and poverty.

> The best-intentioned CETA programs disappointed those of us who created and funded them, and frustrated those who expected meaningful employment skills and well-paying jobs. On thousands of street corners, unemployed CETA graduates mingle

70

with thousands of other jobless men and women. Their training turned out to be irrelevant or inadequate for local employers who advertise in vain for the craftsmen they need.[85]

Training programs can be useful if job opportunities exist for the training they provide, and it is clear from the sorry history of government programs that it is very difficult to match the training with the job market. But many people would argue that, in any case, the best form of job training is usually to start at the bottom in a small company. It may not be glamorous, or well paid, but it provides the opportunity to gain experience and to demonstrate reliability. Credentials of this nature are usually much more valuable than certificates from any number of government training programs. Perhaps we should spend more time and money encouraging the creation of more first-rung jobs for people in depressed neighborhoods, by improving the climate for new business, and enable them to start climbing the employment ladder, and less trying in vain to start them halfway up the ladder.

The dismal lack of success of government measures seeking to stimulate employment in distressed areas fits the general pattern of programs aimed at revitalizing depressed urban neighborhoods. Minimum wages, like rent control and public housing projects, seem to have aggravated the problems they were designed to solve. CETA programs, like housing subsidies, have achieved very marginal improvements at enormous cost. The successes are few, and the failures legion.

It is clear that if our aim in urban policy is to reverse the unnecessary decline of neighborhoods, we are not achieving that goal by the policies we are now pursuing. We pour billions of dollars into the cities, and yet the gap between rich and poor neighborhoods is actually increasing. This divergence can lead only to more explosions of the kind we saw in Watts and Liberty City.

Let us try to stop doing the things that are destroying the cities. This would be a great leap forward. But we must also devise policies that fit the characteristics of neighborhoods and the communities that live in them, rather than the planner's perception of what they should be. If we do this, and if we try to activate and build on the latent strengths of communities in depressed areas, we may set in motion a process of self-improvement. At the moment, we seem only to frustrate enthusiasm and enterprise where they are needed most of all.

71

NOTES

1. *Washington Post,* 14 May 1980.
2. George Peterson, "Finance," in William Gorham and Nathan Glazer, *The Urban Predicament* (The Urban Institute, Washington, D.C., 1976), p. 81.
3. Joel Haveman and Rochelle Stanfield, " 'Neutral' Federal Policies: Are They Reducing Frostbelt-Sunbelt Spending Imbalances?" *National Journal,* 7 February 1981, p. 234.
4. Peterson, "Finance," p. 60.
5. *National Journal,* 24 May 1980, p. 844.
6. *Washington Post,* 27 December 1979.
7. *Ibid.*
8. David Schulz, Assistant Director of the Chicago capital budget, *National Journal,* 24 May 1980, p. 844.
9. *Ibid.,* p. 846.
10. *Ibid.*
11. Peterson, "Finance," pp. 64-65.
12. Eugene Meehan, *Public Housing, Conventin Versus Reality* (Center for Urban Policy Research, New Brunswick, New Jersey, 1975), pp. 77-78.
13. Quoted in Neal Peirce, "Planning the City," *Baltimore Sun,* 20 October 1980.
14. *Ibid.*
15. Jane Jacobs, *The Death and Life of Great American Cities* (Random House, New York, 1961), p. 4.
16. *The New York Times,* 13 June 1980.
17. *Wall Street Journal,* 13 November 1980.
18. *Ibid.*
19. John Weicher, *Housing Policies and Programs* (American Enterprise Institute, Washington, D.C., 1980). Weicher's book provides an excellent survey of the federal role in housing.
20. *Ibid.,* p. 25.
21. *Ibid.,* p. 1.
22. For a review of the effects of the Davis-Bacon Act, see Weicher, *Housing Policies,* pp. 55-56; John Gould, *Davis-Bacon Act: The Economies of Prevailing Wage Laws* (American Enterprise Institute, Washington, D.C., 1971).
23. Comptroller General, GAO, *The Need for Improved Administration of the Davis-Bacon Act* (USGPO, Washington, D.C., 1971).
24. Richard Muth, *Public Housing: An Economic Evaluation* (American Enterprise Institute, Washington, D.C., 1973), p. 13.
25. Weicher, *Housing Policies,* p. 59.
26. *Ibid.,* p. 60.
27. *Ibid.*
28. Stuart Butler, *Government Intervention in the Housing Market in Britain* (The Heritage Foundation, Washington, D.C., 1978), pp. 13-14.
29. Robert Sadacca et al., *Management Performance in Public Housing* (Urban Institute, Washington, D.C., 1974), pp. 31-32.
30. Weicher, *Housing Policies,* p. 65.
31. *Ibid.,* p. 47.
32. Donald Robinson, "Billion-Dollar Nightmare at HUD," *Reader's Digest,* June 1980, p. 129.
33. *Ibid.,* p. 130.
34. *Ibid.,* p. 131.
35. Weicher, *Housing Policies,* p. 79.

36. U.S. Congressional Budget Office, *The Long-Term Costs of Lower-Income Housing Assistance Programs* (USGPO, Washington, D.C., 1979), pp. 21-25.
37. U.S. Bureau of the Census, *Market Absorption of Apartments, Annual:1979 Absorption* (Current Housing Report, Series H-130-79-5, 1980).
38. Weicher, *Housing Policies*, p. 69.
39. U.S. Congressional Budget Office, *Federal Housing Policy* (USGPO, Washington, D.C., 1978), p. 28.
40. Weicher, *Housing Policies*, p. 159.
41. *New York Times*, 27 December 1979.
42. *Ibid.*
43. *National Journal*, 17 February 1979, p. 264.
44. *Ibid.*
45. Eric Hemel, "What Does Rent Control Control?", *Taxes and Spending* (Institute for Contemporary Studies, San Francisco), Fall 1979, p. 85.
46. *Wall Street Journal*, 1 February 1980.
47. F. G. Pennance, in *Rent Control: A Popular Paradox* (Fraser Institute, Vancouver, B.C., 1975), pp. 63-64.
48. Department of the Environment, *Housing Policy Manual* (HMSO, London, England, 1977), p. 67.
49. Butler, *Government Intervention*, p. 11.
50. Quoted in Thomas Haslett, "The New York Disease," *Inquiry,* 26 May 1980, p. 18.
51. *Wall Street Journal,* 1 February 1980.
52. *Washington Post*, 3 November 1980.
53. Walter Williams, *Obstacles to Slum Neighborhood Revitalization* (Temple University, Philadelphia, 1978).
54. U.S. Department of Housing and Urban Development, *Final Report of the Task Force on Housing Costs* (USGPO, Washington, D.C., 1978), p. 35.
55. U.S. Department of Housing and Urban Development, *Housing Cost Reduction Demonstration* (USGPO, Washington, D.C., 1980).
56. *Berkeley Daily Gazette,* 30 September 1978, noted in Charles Baird, *Rent Control: The Perennial Folly* (CATO Institute, San Francisco, 1980), p. 37.
57. Stephen Seidel, *Housing Costs and Government Regulation* (Center for Urban Policy Research, New Brunswick, New Jersey, 1978), pp. 32-35.
58. *Wall Street Journal,* 11 October 1978.
59. For an analysis of the impact of zoning, see Michael Goldberg and Peter Howard, *Zoning: Its Costs and Relevance for the 1980s* (Fraser Institute, Vancouver, B.C., 1980).
60. See Bernard Siegan, *Land Without Zoning* (Lexington Books, Lexington, Mass., 1973); Siegan, "No Zoning Is the Best Zoning," in Benjamin Bobo et al., *No Land Is an Island* (Institute for Contemporary Studies, San Francisco, 1975); and Roscoe Jones, "Houston: City Planning Without Zoning," in Goldberg and Howard, *Zoning.*
61. Siegan, "No Zoning," p. 158.
62. Jones, "Houston," p. 48.
63. *Ibid.,* p. 50.
64. Joint Economic Committee of the U.S. Congress, *Central City Businesses—Plans and Problems* (U.S. Congress, Washington, D.C., 1979). Prepared for the Subcommittee on Fiscal and Intergovernmental Policy. The cities selected for the survey were Atlanta, Dallas, Detroit, Los Angeles, Minneapolis, New York, Phoenix, Pittsburgh, Seattle and St. Louis.
65. Quoted in *Nation's Business*, March 1980, p. 72.

66. Murray Weidenbaum, *The Future of Business Regulation* (Amacom, New York, 1980), p. 52.
67. *Fortune,* November 1979, p. 96.
68. *Ibid.,* p. 94.
69. *Fortune,* November 1975, p. 145.
70. J.E.C., *Central City Businesses,* p. 23.
71. *Ibid.,* p. 17.
72. *Ibid.,* p. 10.
73. *Ibid.,* p. 4.
74. Susan Jacobs and Elizabeth Roistacher, "The Urban Impacts of HUD's Development Action Grant Program," in Norman Glickman (ed.), *The Urban Impacts of Federal Policies* (Johns Hopkins University Press, Baltimore, 1980), p. 348.
75. *Business Week*, 12 November 1979, p. 147.
76. Robert Poole, "Community and Regional Development," in Eugene McAllister (ed.), *Agenda for Progress* (The Heritage Foundation, Washington, D.C., 1981), p. 181.
77. *Ibid.,* p. 186.
78. *Wall Street Journal*, 12 March 1980.
79. *Washington Post*, 24 September 1980.
80. *Ibid.*
81. David Birch, *The Job Generation Process* (MIT Press, Cambridge, Mass., 1979), pp. 17, 20.
82. National Federation of Independent Business, unpublished survey, Washington, D.C., 1979.
83. Walter Williams, "Government Sanctioned Restraints That Reduce Economic Opportunities for Minorities," *Policy Review*, Fall 1977, p. 14.
84. *Wall Street Journal*, 12 November 1980.
85. *Washington Post*, 12 December 1980.

3. THE FOUNDATIONS OF THE ENTERPRISE ZONE

Job Creation in the Inner Cities

As the shortcomings of conventional urban policies have become more obvious, there has emerged in both Europe and America a strong body of thought urging a quite different approach to the problems of the inner cities. In a 1977 editorial, the London *Times* described what it perceived to be a clear move away from the interventionist urban planning philosophy of the 1960s:

> Protestations are not always a safe guide to performance, of course, but out of the current outpourings of official and unofficial comment on the problems of the inner cities some signs of a concensus have appeared. It is a concensus shaped partly by a faltering confidence in the effectiveness of grand designs—let alone the availability of money to finance them. . . . But it is also partly formed by repentance for past errors....
>
> Now the emphasis is rightly on rehabilitation, encouragement of small industry, discouragement of motorways, and respect for community structures.[1]

As *The Times* observed, there are two principal elements of what one might call the rethinking on urban policy. There is the growing appreciation that radical physical change in a community might well do more harm than good, because it breaks up the intangible, but real, social bonds that are vital to the life of a

75

neighborhood, and it imposes on the area a planner's vision of how people behave—which may be very different from the way they do. This understanding that disruption may be fatal to a community has spurred the trend toward rehabilitation, and the whole approach of building on the strengths of a neighborhood—rather than tearing down its buildings and replacing them.

The second element noted by *The Times* concerns the better understanding both of the relative importance of job creation in inner cities, compared with housing creation, and the nature of the job-generation process. Although it would be quite wrong, of course, to suggest that planners and politicians have paid no attention to employment creation in the inner cities, it would be true to say that there has been an overemphasis on rebuilding. The assumption seems to have been that one needs to improve the housing and other buildings in a neighborhood *before* significant economic activity can be expected. Yet, as we see in neighborhood after neighborhood, mass unemployment is rarely cured by putting the unemployed in new houses, and a failure to generate jobs in a community will lead to the deterioration of rebuilt areas—no matter how many design prizes they receive.

Not only is job creation seen as the chief priority by the "concensus" detected by *The Times*, but the role of the private sector as the provider of jobs is central to recent thinking. Improvements in the physical structures in a neighborhood will result from the employment and optimism that flow from an expansion of the private business sector, and a policy that considers rebuilding as the chief priority is putting the cart before the horse. Rather, the emphasis should be on encouraging the small business sector that was once the economic heart of the major cities.

The importance of stimulating the entrepreneurial spirit of the small businessman, as a means of restoring the health of the inner cities, is accepted across much of the political spectrum. Even British social democrats, such as Joe Rogaly of the London *Financial Times*, stress the need to attract small workshops back into the blighted areas of cities:

> State policies have failed: let capitalism have its chance....Solid recovery can best be provided by increasing the number of jobs available, and one way to do that is to stimulate an increase in the number of small businesses—service as well as manufacturing— operating in such areas or near enough to make a bus or

underground ride to work worth considering. The state can huff and puff, but apart from removing restrictions and reducing taxes it cannot really achieve this: capitalists are the best people to spawn capitalists.[2]

A great deal of attention has been given to the job-creating characteristics of smaller businesses in recent years. Part of this attention in the United States has been due to very extensive and significant work by David Birch of the Massachusetts Institute of Technology. Birch examined 5.6 million businesses, representing 80% of all private sector employment, and analyzed the job creating powers of those businesses over a test period, breaking them down by size, region, and other variables.

Birch's findings are important, and remarkable, not only from a research perspective, but also for the clear implications they have for urban policy. He found that for the country as a whole, firms with 20 or fewer employees generated 66% of all net new private sector jobs in the period under study (1969-76). Almost four-fifths of these small sector jobs were provided by independent, free-standing entrepreneurs—as distinct from small branches of larger companies.[3] On a regional basis, the pattern was even more dramatic. In the Northeast, small firms (0-20 employees) accounted as a sector for virtually *all* the net new jobs created. Firms with 21-50 employees did show a small net increase in employment, but all size groups larger than that registered substantial net employment losses—companies with more than 100 employees suffered a net loss of one-third of their total work force. Larger companies did make a contribution to new job creation in the South and West, but even in these regions the small sector provided 54% and 60% respectively of all the net new jobs generated.

Birch pointed out that most of the new jobs that are created come from young firms—80% of all replacement jobs provided during the period came from firms that were less than four years old. This pattern held across all sectors of the economy and across all regions. These young firms do tend to be fragile—65% of small firms were found to fail within the first four years. But Birch also found that among the firms that do survive the high-risk early period of their lives, small companies were four times more likely to expand than contract. Larger firms, on the other hand, proved to be 50% more likely to shrink than grow. Volatility (i.e., instability) appeared to be an essential characteristic of strong job generation. "The biggest gainers of all, curiously but consistently," Birch found,

> are establishments that declined the most during the recent past, but survived. These establishments have a higher than average expectation of dying, but, if they make it, they are the ones most likely to generate a large number of new jobs in the future. On balance, they are in fact two or three times more likely to be large job generators." [4]

There were equally surprising results when Birch compared the rates of job loss and job creation from region to region. The rate of loss due to closures or contractions was found to be the same everywhere—approximately 8% per year. The Frostbelt was not found to be losing jobs from existing firms any faster than the Sunbelt, nor were cities actually losing jobs any faster than the suburbs. The "deathrate" of jobs seemed to be remarkably constant. There were significant differences, however, in the rate at which jobs were created through start-ups and expansions. Cities and certain regions suffered a net decline in jobs because of a low "birthrate" of companies and employment, not because the deathrate of jobs was particularly high. Job *replacement* is the key factor, Birch discovered, not job loss.

In a recent study using the same data, Birch carried out a comparative analysis of employment generation and loss within different parts of ten selected metropolitan areas. The ten cities were grouped according to the following charactertics:

Group Label	*Group Characteristics*	*Group Cities*
Fast	Central city growing	Charlotte, SC
	Metropolitan area growing	Houston, TX
Moderate	Central city declining	Hartford, CT
	Metropolitan area growing	Baltimore, MD
		Boston, MA
		Rochester, NY
		Dayton, OH
Declining	Central city declining	New Haven, CT
	Metropolitan area declining	Worcester, MA
		Greenville, SC

There was very little difference in the rate of job loss among the cities examined, or between the central cities and the suburbs.

Indeed, the small variation that did exist was the exact opposite of what most people would have expected. It was the fastest growing city, Houston, that experienced the highest rate of job loss due to closures and contractions over the period covered (1972-76). The lowest rate of job loss was in Worcester, a declining city.[5] "This is not a paradox," wrote Birch:

> It simply reflects the fact that the healthier an economy is, in the job generation sense, the more active it is and the more its corporate population is turning over. Turnover is a natural consequence of entrepreneurial activity. Those who would reduce deaths as a way of improving the health of an economy clearly misunderstand the processes that lead to job creation.[6]

The clear pattern that emerges from Birch's findings is that the older and less vigorous an area is—either a whole city or a neighborhood within it—the more it depends on smaller businesses, particularly in the service sector, to generate employment. In order to improve the employment situation within these areas, we should be encouraging the establishment of larger numbers of small firms, rather than trying to hold on to old ones, or attempting to attract large companies. Development strategies aimed at saving employment by reducing the loss rate, says Birch, are "as futile as telling the tide not to go out."

The most effective job creators, argues Birch, are the most difficult businesses for government to reach or deal with. The risks involved in funding them with grants and loans are very high, even if they can be persuaded to meet the terms of government support. But as Birch and many others point out, these small entrepreneurs state loudly and frequently that they want less government involvement in their business lives, not more. Rather than new loans and grants, the cry is for less regulation and lower taxation.

The conclusions must be, as Birch argues, that direct aid for the purposes of inner-city employment, would be far better used as a form of short-term assistance to medium and larger companies that are faced with the pressure to lay off workers. Even this kind of support has a habit of becoming permanent assistance without the saving of many jobs. Whatever one's view of this type of support, however, it is clear from the MIT study's findings that it can do little more than make a marginal difference to employment levels in a city. "What the data do show," writes Birch, is that cities that wish to capitalize upon the job-generating powers of smaller businesses within their boundaries are going to have to complement the traditional economic development vehicles with a broader approach. They must come to understand the special needs of the entrepreneur. They must work with their state legislatures to develop indirect tax and regulatory strategies that foster the "percolation" of thousands of small businesses at the same time that they work on the politically more satisfying task of handing out money directly.[7]

The clear message is that government would be far more effective at creating jobs in the inner cities if it sought to improve the entrepreneurial climate of small businesses; to improve the birthrate of firms instead of trying to reduce the loss rate of companies. And this whole approach would be more rewarding than seeking to lure major corporations into depressed areas.

There is strong evidence from other sources, and other countries, that suggests this would be a better approach. It is interesting to note, for example, that Britain has been suffering from poor economic growth for many years, and that it has one of the weakest small business sectors in the western industrialized world. "A strong small business sector," notes the London *Economist*, "is closely related to economic growth." Yet British governments have tended to maintain a very perverse climate for such firms:

Small businesses have always relied heavily, especially at the start, on investment by the owner, his family, and friends. High direct tax rates have hindered modern-day Aunt Agathas and their nephews from accumulating capital to invest, while tax reliefs on pensions, insurance, and government bonds have channelled what they do manage to save into institutions prevented by law from investing it in small firms.[8]

The observations of *The Economist* indicate that the need for an improved small-business climate is just as necessary in Britain as in the United States, and that the nature of small enterprise is very similar. It was mentioned in the previous chapter that a survey by NFIB indicated that 60% of small American firms start with savings and personal loans forming the principal source of finance. A study of the foreign literature by Albert Shapiro has shown that the same pattern holds true in most countries. Private investment and trade credit are the major sources of new enterprise capital throughout the world. Banks, investment funds, and government agencies rarely play much of a role in small business creation.[9] Even venture-capital firms account for only a tiny fraction of start-ups— just 0.3% in NFIB's survey of principal sources of finance.

It is customary, of course, to assume that much of the problem in poor areas is that banks will not lend to entrepreneurs. Although some banks may be short-sighted, for the most part they are very wise *not* to lend in such neighborhoods—especially to small new companies. Such would-be borrowers have little or no track record in business, and the chances of failure for any number of reasons is very high. Furthermore, the overhead cost of making the small loans required can be very uneconomical for banks, considering the risk of default. Banks invest the money in careful savers; they are not suitable vehicles for high-risk loans.

Private channels of small business capital, on the other hand, are often considered "inefficient" from an accountant's point of view. There are few small businessmen who can honestly say that the risk and probable return they faced really justified their initial investment, compared with the alternatives available. More often they and their friends invest in the firm for less tangible reasons than the purely monetary return that might ensue. They want to be their own boss, or they want the freedom to do work that they like, and they convince themselves as well as their friends that they can also make some money. As Albert Shapiro points out, the prime motivation is often more negative than positive—the buildup of frustration with one's present job and its prospects, or even the loss of a job.[10]

It would be difficult to justify either encouraging or requiring commercial banks (that administer the money of cautious people) or government agencies (who distribute the money of equally cautious taxpayers) to invest in such high-risk enterprises in uninviting city neighborhoods. More sensible would be a tax policy aimed at providing greater incentives for the entrepreneur to save and take risks, and a reduction in the unnecessary tax and regulatory obstacles that both increase the capital he must find, and cause him so often to give up, fail, or never even try.

The importance of the small businessman is not confined simply to the number of jobs he can create in the inner city. He is a different type of businessman than the executive of a large corporation. In general, he will have at least some knowledge of business, gained usually from working for another company—more often than not another *small* company.[11] He will probably have very little capital, but he will offset this with a willingness to substitute his own labor for "capital," by carrying out modifications to the business premises himself; and he will tend to plow back earnings into the company rather than putting them into his own pocket. He will also be prepared to work long hours to enable his company to grow—or to survive. A survey of its small business members by NFIB revealed that almost 80% of them worked an average of 49 hours a week, and 14% worked over 72 hours.[12]

These kinds of entrepreneurs are very suitable for the inner-city environment, where conditions are often far from ideal. They are more adaptable and innovative, and they are flexible enough to make do with less than ideal buildings, infrastructure, and facilities. A new, small company can often open in a basement, a disused warehouse, a garage, or even temporary buildings on a rubble-strewn lot—if it is allowed to do so. When it grows larger it may well move elsewhere for more space and a better environment. But there are always other people with ideas who can take its place if given the opportunity.

This "make do" characteristic of small businessmen not only makes them suitable for poor, inner-city neighborhoods, but, as Jane Jacobs has explained, it makes the older neighborhoods more suitable for the businesses. Large, successful companies with known markets and tested products tend to establish in new, expensive structures. They need them, can afford them, and can carry the risk of a heavy long-term commitment. New, small, high-risk companies, on the other hand, need low overheads to survive, and they rarely need custom-built facilities or well-maintained city infrastructure to make a location attractive to them. New companies, writes Mrs. Jacobs,

> can make out successfully in old buildings, but they are inexorably slain by the overhead of new construction.
>
> As for really new ideas of any kind—no matter how ultimately profitable or otherwise successful they might be—there is no leeway for such chancy trial, error and experimentation in the high overhead economy of new construction. Old ideas can sometimes use new buildings. New ideas must use old buildings.[13]

82

Regrettably, through zoning, high property taxes, a multitude of permits, building codes, and the other paraphernalia of government, we have gradually made even old buildings too expensive for new ventures.

The small entrepreneur is well suited to the kind of work force that exists in the inner cities, as well as to the buildings of the neighborhood. In a new small company, the owner and his family usually compose the entire staff of the business. The proprietor will be both accountant and floorsweeper. But as the business grows, the demand also grows for outside labor to free the owner from unskilled, time-consuming tasks so that he can concentrate on the technical aspects of his expanding firm.

The employment opportunities that open up as a result of this process are exactly the ones that are most appropriate for the young, unskilled work force of the inner city. Although the jobs are low skilled and low paid, they are not the same as unskilled jobs in a large hotel or a manufacturing company. They have much more potential for upward mobility. The unskilled workers in a small company have more opportunity to learn the operation of the business, and to acquire the skills and experience that are necessary to grow with the company, taking more responsible, better paid positions that become available as the firm expands. If the firm collapses, or stagnates, the employees have at least gained experience that makes them more attractive to another company that is growing. A growing small sector is quite different in the opportunity it provides for low-skilled workers than is generally the case in the large-company sector. The hierarchy is less rigid, less dependent on paper qualifications, and based far more on proven reliability.

In her book *The Economy of Cities*, Jane Jacobs discusses the importance of small-business flexibility and innovation to cities as a whole, not merely to neighborhoods within a city. In order to illustrate her theme, she draws a comparison between two English cities. Manchester was the most "efficient" and advanced industrial city in England in the mid-19th century. Huge textile mills dominated the economy as well as the landscape. Manchester showed a clear sense of direction—almost of purpose. Birmingham, on the other hand, was then a city of small workshops, overlapping work and duplication. People would leave businesses and set up for themselves. Compared with Manchester, Birmingham seemed a very muddled city. It did not know where it was going.

But today, Manchester is in the grip of decline. The industries that provided its foundation are now obsolete and their markets have disappeared. Like many other symbols of Victorian urban strength, Manchester was so "efficient" that it could not adapt to change. Birmingham, in contrast, found that its muddle of small entrepreneurs could adjust to change and seize the opportunities that the change offered. Like London, which has never specialized, Birmingham has been able to grow and prosper.[14]

We might learn some lessons from this for cities in general. We need look only to Detroit to see America's Manchester. Cities that depend on a single industry, with the local economy geared to it, are very successful as long as that industry is growing. But if there is a dramatic upheaval in the industry's market, or in the economics of production that affect the city's competitiveness, the effect can be cataclysmic.

If the change in the market is temporary, then recovery can, of course, take place. But if it is fundamental and sustained, the city can recover only by altering its economic base through the development of new companies in new industries. City planners have a habit of assuming that means by trying to lure large new companies to replace the dying ones. But they soon find that it is no easy task to find corporations that will match the characteristics of the city and its labor force, or to persuade them, if found, to move into the city.

When rapid recovery does take place, it is invariably due to the trial-and-error process of small-scale enterprise rather than to centrally planned changes. Los Angeles is a particularly interesting example of this process in action. That city experienced the common economic paradox of war. Aircraft manufacturing, shipbuilding, and other industries became central to the city's economy during World War II. But when peace came, these industries practically collapsed, and hundreds of thousands of workers were laid off. Yet within four years a dramatic economic recovery had taken place.

What happened was that a remarkable expansion took place in the number of new business starts. These businesses were often established by laid-off workers, and many were formed in garages, basements, and lofts. They grew rapidly in number and in output;

and they produced a remarkable range of goods and services, many of which were substitutes for goods previously imported into the city. During the second half of the 1940s, according to Jane Jacobs, one-eighth of all the new businesses in the entire United States were started in Los Angeles.[15] Many failed, but the others formed the base for a sustained recovery of the city.

Today the practice in Europe, and increasingly in America, is to try to stem the decline of a city's traditional industries by subsidizing them out of the public purse, instead of accepting change and establishing the entrepreneurial climate necessary for the rapid development of new businesses. It is a policy that is humanitarian in instinct but misguided in practice. Nobody likes to see giant plants closed down and working people made idle. But invariably the policy of government support leads to less efficiency and competitiveness, and ever-larger subsidies merely to maintain the same level of employment. Labor and capital are locked into the supported industry, and are denied to those who might grow in its place. When the collapse finally does come, it is all the more calamitous because the industry has become even more obsolete. And the task of new businesses is even greater than it should have been.

Understanding Neighborhoods

In addition to the growing realization, in America at least, that the small business sector is crucial to the economic revival of the inner cities, there has also been a shift away from an emphasis on rebuilding in favor of the renovation of existing structures. On both sides of the Atlantic, according to Jean Mestres of the Council of International Urban Liaison, we can see "the demise of the bulldozer approach to urban renewal and its replacement by scaled down strategies responsive to human needs."[16]

Part of the reason for this change of heart is the simple realization that tearing down large chunks of our cities and rebuilding them has not improved them, and that in many cases it may have hastened their decline. But beyond this cost-benefit conclusion a greater understanding can be seen among policy-makers of the way in which older neighborhoods function and how subtle forces tie their residents together.

Much of the credit for this greater appreciation of the way in which neighborhoods function must be given to Jane Jacobs. Her book *The Death and Life of Great American Cities*[17] was a key factor in the erosion of the consensus that had led to many of the urban planning disasters of the 1950s and 1960s. The book grew out of her keen and perceptive observations of urban communities and the social forces that operate within them. She has been both applauded and condemned. But her work set in motion an examination of the anatomy of neighborhoods that has contributed significantly to the shift in thinking.

The principal theme of Mrs. Jacobs's work is that *diversity* is crucial for an inner city neighborhood to be strong and vibrant. This diversity may seem to the casual observer to be chaos, but it leads to a subtle order arising out of the complex interplay of social and economic activities within the community. This order, based on diversity, contributes to the vitality and safety that is the foundation of all successful communities.

Mrs. Jacobs identifies four essential conditions for diversity. When developers and planners ignore these conditions, she argues, they are condemning even the most elegant and ambitious plans to failure.

The first condition that must be met, she writes, is that there must be a mixture of "primary users." In other words, people must be in the streets for different purposes at different times. If this is not the case, streets in the neighborhood will become deserted and threatening. The mixed use of buildings, in order to allow various users to exist side by side, is often absent as a feature of development plans, and many local zoning ordinances are explicitly designed to prevent it—supposedly for the good of the community!

The continuous presence of people in the streets, for various purposes, is essential for the safety of the neighborhood, and this in turn is a necessary foundation for economic improvement. People in the street, and in the business premises adjacent to it, means the continous surveillance of the street. This is a greater deterrent to crime than any number of police cruisers. The mixed use of buildings contributes to this continuous activity in the neighborhood. A school will bring mothers and children into the streets in the mornings and late afternoons. A small factory will provide pedestrians at lunchtime, with the constant movement of people related to the business. A cafe, even a launderette, provides a "watchtower" on the street throughout the day. Mixed use of the buildings does not *guarantee* a reduction in crime: A bar, and even a school, may actually generate vandalism and more serious crimes. But as a general rule, the more varied the activities in the street, the safer it will be.

The mixed use of buildings within a block leads to an additional benefit if there are a number of small businessmen present. The small shopkeeper or workshop owner is one of the "public characters" (as Jane Jacobs calls them) who form the public link between the otherwise private residents of the neighborhood. They are the binding force within the community, and are often the self-appointed, but accepted, leaders of it. They will complain—and will know how to—when a pothole appears in the street. They will notice when the elderly resident across the street does not pick up her paper, and will check to see all is well. Perhaps most important of all, they have a direct stake in the neighborhood, and they will want to keep it safe for their property and their customers—and hence for all residents. When trouble breaks out they will intervene or call the police. It is interesting to note that in the movie *Fort Apache, The Bronx*, the *only* person who was prepared to tackle a violent criminal, other than the police, was a middle-aged shopkeeper wielding a broom. The movie might be justly criticized for its portrayal of the inhabitants of the South Bronx, but it is quite accurate in its appreciation of the protective function of the shopkeeper. The existence of public characters such as shopkeepers and other businessmen is an essential part of a safe neighborhood.

A recent article in *The New York Times* illustrates the difference that can be made when public characters and the residents of an area work together. The article dealt with the Belmont district of the South Bronx, a neighborhood of 25,000 people that is an oasis in what has become the national symbol of urban decay.[18] The district contributes to about one-third of the population of New York's 48th police precinct, and yet accounts for only 9% of the precinct's crime. Murders, robberies and other crimes equal a tiny fraction of those in adjoining neighborhoods.

The key to success in the Belmont district has been that churchmen, businessmen, and the residents of the community form a tight but informal network that forms a strong barrier against crime. "You have an involved community," says one policeman, "and it's difficult for a man to come in and commit a crime without being spotted." A detective pointed out, "The police are only as good as the eyes and ears of the people, and that's why things work so well here."

Around the business area of Belmont, in particular, there is a strong sense of safety. There are few bars or steel grates on the windows of the Italian bakeries and other shops that form the base of the district, and people are in the streets deep into the night. That *sense* of safety, which results from the combined influence of the public characters and the residents themselves, contributes to the *reality* of safety. "People are out in the day and the night because they feel safe," explains one policeman, "and because people are always out it *is* safe."

The importance of the public character and mixed land use has been seen increasingly in recent years as a key element in successful community development. The HUD-sponsored Council on Development Choices, drawn from a wide range of development specialists and elected officials, noted this in its 1980 report. The Council urged that there should be an end to the practice of fifty years, whereby "communities have worked to segregate the recreation and shopping; all in the interest of separating so-called 'incompatible' uses."[19] The Council argued strongly that zoning and other restrictions should be modified substantially to allow a mix of building uses. The aim should be the encouragement of what the Council called "urban villages," where different aspects of urban life could exist together. The idea of the urban village is applicable to many locations, it was argued, but

> Perhaps the most important opportunities are in older cities. Existing built-up areas may be revitalized by expanding or reorganizing use arrangements or providing new uses to give a focus to collections of fragmented neighborhoods....A major purpose of applying the Urban Village concept should be to provide major employment centers for existing residents, especially minorities and the poor.[20]

The two other basic requirements for diversity, according to Jane Jacobs, are related to the type and the layout of buildings in a neighborhood. There must be a mixture of old and new buildings. As already explained, the principal reason for this is to provide the mixture of facilities needed for both small, embryonic firms and more established, larger companies. Mixed use is often impossible without mixed age. And similarly, it is necessary to have housing of varying prices if a beneficial mix of residents is to be found in the community. In addition, she argues, city blocks should be short, so that alternative thoroughfares are created for pedestrians to meet, and for them to find and patronize businesses. When there are only long blocks in a district, pedestrians and vehicles tend to gravitate to particular well-used streets, leaving others as exitless, deserted, and threatening sections of the neighborhood. They invite the insecurity and crime that undermine the community.

The fourth condition for diversity, writes Mrs. Jacobs, is that there must be a dense concentration of population within the neighborhood, including workers and visitors as well as residents. It is a fallacy, she argues, to equate high concentration with social problems, and to assume that it is synonymous with overcrowding. A high concentration is needed to provide a flourishing street life for the neighborhood, and to support the economic base of the community. The idea that what poor areas need is more open space, fountains, and parking lots—rather than people—could not be further from the truth.

Mrs. Jacobs contends that these conditions are essential for neighborhood vitality. Individually, they may not lead to the diversity that is necessary for a strong community, but in combination they provide the foundation. Yet the development projects rarely combine these features. The segregation of residential and business districts has been a standard feature of zoning and most projects in depressed areas. The layout of streets is normally seen only as a mechanism for moving people efficiently from one place to another. The idea of a street as a means of encouraging social communication and a sense of safety tends to be overlooked. And until very recently, it was almost automatically assumed that *new* was by definition better than old. In city after city, we have seen old buildings, housing small, local businesses and low-income people, torn down to make way for impressive new buildings that are unsuitable or too costly for people they displaced.

In recent years there has also been a growing appreciation of the role and potential of neighborhood organizations as a means of providing services within a community. Somehow, the importance of such informal groups was forgotten when the armchair humanitarians began to plan the lives of the inner-city poor. It was assumed that people in poor neighborhoods are in some way impotent, either unwilling or unable to deal with many of the problems their communities face. If crime was to be reduced, and welfare provided, then some level of government had to take responsibility. This philosophy gave rise not only to enormous expenditures with questionable effects on the recipients, but led also to the emergence of well-organized intermediaries and professional welfare groups that Robert Woodson has described as the "social welfare complex": "This layer of professionals has become a sponge that absorbs society's money and good will without passing it on to the people society has undertaken to help."[21]

Woodson argues that the inability of such professionals to demonstrate significant improvements in many neighborhoods has not caused people to conclude that they are the wrong people for the job, but rather that the urban poor are beyond hope, and should be considered as a permanently dependent underclass. But, says Woodson: "Our domestic policy makers, captured by the social welfare/poverty complex, have been going to the wrong places for answers. They have ignored those closest to the problem, those who have demonstrated success in addressing some of the most depressing difficulties in urban neighborhoods: the grassroots community leaders."[22]

These community leaders, like many of the small business people and church leaders, are among the "public characters" of a neighborhood. They are at the heart of the informal network that can help to make an area self-reliant, and can generate the kind of services that most well-meaning outsiders believe can come only from government. Such groups have organized crime-watch programs and block patrols, leading to a significant reduction in crime in many locations. They are effective not merely because they provide eyes for the conventional sources of security, but rather because they are *of* the community. They are trusted. They are not seen as some outside force or provider, but as people who are firmly rooted in the neighborhood. "Such community groups," writes Woodson:

> take on functions historically assigned to families. They mediate between the community and its youths and, in so doing, truly modify the young people, many of whom have been the "scandal"

of juvenile justice programs. They draw the community youths into positive, reconstructive activities that serve the needs of the community while enabling the youths to recognize and accept new, positive ways of being themselves in their own neighborhoods, among their own people.[23]

Woodson points out that groups of this kind can achieve remarkable results with minimal resources and professional training. As an example, he describes the House of Umoja in Philadelphia, which over a period of ten years has transformed more than five hundred alienated young minority men, many of whom had been gang members, into productive citizens.[24] By acting as an extended family within the community, the House was able to provide the support that many violent young people needed and wanted. Its activities had a decisive effect on youth crime in the city.

Other groups in other cities have provided the same form of "social infrastructure" for neighborhoods, and have achieved a much greater impact than has usually been the case with well-trained professionals. Such groups do not confine their activities to crime and welfare matters, however. Many engage in revitalization projects, often in cooperation with charitable institutions and other nongovernmental bodies. Sometimes the most unlikely people are drawn into such local projects. In East Harlem, for instance, the Pratt Institute was able to work with one of the district's gangs to develop of plan to renovate a twelve block area.[25]

Local initiatives can have a profound impact on a neighborhood. According to Neal Peirce, a leading urban affairs writer:

> The results are often little short of phenomenal. When residents of an endangered apartment building or neighborhood realize that they can make decisions for themselves, attitudes change abruptly. Crime, vandalism and drug usage plummet. Buildings that police once feared to enter suddenly become self-policing. Self-help community groups, in the words of Ron Shiffman, director of the Pratt Institute's Center for Community and Environmental Development, begin to evidence "the same pioneering spirit that built so many communities across the country."[26]

Freedom is essential to the success of these groups. They cannot be innovative and responsive if they have to meet guidelines and codes that have no relevance to the problems of the area. They can be pioneering only if, like the early pioneers, they are allowed to be flexible. The last thing a community group needs is to be noticed by government. When "officials" become impressed with a group's results and take an interest in it, the freedom and flexibility the group needs has a habit of disappearing. The House of Umoja faced just such a problem, according to one of its founders, Sister Falaka Fattah:

> Because we have a residential program, which is a group house, now we have to deal with a license every year. Before we were "discovered " we were doing the same job without a license.
>
> In order to have a license, you have to pass the different [regulations]...the kitchen has to be just so; you have to have a social worker. They tell you your house has to be fixed up, but they don't give you any money to fix it up. It's a bureaucratic nightmare.[27]

The House of Umoja has survived, but other successful groups have been regularized out of existence. Government tries to be protective. It tries to ensure that people under the care of organizations can be sure that facilities meet basic standards, and it seeks to ensure that block patrols do not turn into trigger-happy vigilante squads. But the issue is usually not whether people in a blighted area should or should not have help and protection that meets City Hall's standards. More often than not the question is whether they are going to receive adequate help in any form. Moreover, the standards and regulations that government applies are often totally out of touch with conditions in the area, and with the informal, adaptive approach that groups must apply if they are to be successful.

Two important themes run through much of the recent thinking on urban revitalization. The first is that what often seems the most obvious response to the problems of the inner city often ignores the reality of the situation. David Birch points out, for instance, that policies that seek to retain or attract larger companies into depressed neighborhoods overlook the fact that job *losses* are not the main problem and that larger companies are not in any case the principal creators of new employment. Similarly, programs which replace old buildings with new ones as a matter of course, and keep businesses well away from residential areas, misunderstand the importance of old buildings and mixed land use in a poor district. And welfare policies based on the assumption that poor people are incapable of providing many of their own needs and services fail to appreciate not only that local groups can often do a much better job than government, but also that well-meaning regulation can stifle innovative local approaches.

The second theme concerns freedom. Urban and economic planners have long assumed that a structured, comprehensive plan, together with large doses of public money, will produce a result that is necessarily superior to the "chaos" that seems to characterize dealings between individuals. But the evidence suggests otherwise. Neighborhoods and entrepreneurs are far more vital, creative and responsive to people when the dead hand of government is removed than when it tries to guide them.

If governments wish to encourage the revitalization of urban neighborhoods, the clear message must be that instead of frustrating or trying to replace local initiative and small enterprise, it should promote it. The best way it can do this is not to select those whom it feels to be the most suitable businesses and social middlemen and throw money at them, but simply to dismantle the barriers it has created and then keep out of the way.

NOTES

1. *The Times*, 1 July 1977.
2. *Financial Times*, 29 March 1977.
3. David Birch, *The Job Generation Process* (MIT Press, Cambridge, Mass., 1979), p. 8.
4. *Ibid.*, p. 17.
5. David Birch, *Job Creation in Cities* (MIT Press, Cambridge, Mass., 1980), p. 11.
6. *Ibid.*, p. 12.
7. *Ibid.*, p. 38.
8. *The Economist*, 29 September 1979, p. 105.
9. Albert Shapiro, *The Role of Entrepreneurship in Economic Development at the Less-Than National Level* (Ohio State University, Columbus, 1979), p. 29.
10. Albert Shapiro, *Some Social Dimensions of Entrepreneurship* (Ohio State University, Columbus, Ohio, 1980), p. 11.
11. Unpublished survey, NFIB, Washington, D.C., 1979.
12. *Fact Book on Small Business* (NFIB, Washington, D.C., 1979), p. 65.
13. Jane Jacobs, *The Death and Life of Great American Cities* (Random House, New York, 1961), p. 188.

14. Jane Jacobs, *The Economy of Cities* (Random House, New York, 1969), p. 87.
15. *Ibid.*, p. 153.
16. Quoted in Neal Peirce, "Learning From Europe's Cities," *Perspectives* (German Marshall Fund, Washington, D.C.), June 1979, p. 5.
17. Jane Jacobs, *American Cities*.
18. *The New York Times*, 10 February 1981.
19. U.S. Department of Housing and Urban Development, *Development Choices for the 80s* (USGPO, Washington, D.C., 1980), p. 13.
20. *Ibid.*, p. 22.
21. *The New York Times*, 2 September 1980.
22. *Ibid.*
23. Robert Woodson, *A Summons to Life* (Ballinger, Cambridge, Mass., 1981), p. 106.
24. *Ibid.*, Chapters 3 and 4.
25. *Washington Post*, 30 March 1977.
26. *Ibid.*
27. Quoted in William Raspberry, "Self Help Overruled," *Washington Post*, 6 June 1980.

4. ENTERPRISE ZONES IN BRITAIN

The Enterprise Zone Emerges

It is often difficult for the historian to say with certainty where and when an idea was born. Ideas are rarely created at times and places for the convenience of future investigators. In the formal sense, the term "Enterprise Zone" was publicly unveiled in a speech by Sir Geoffrey Howe, M.P., in June 1978, while he was economics spokesman for the then opposition British Conservative Party. But as Sir Geoffrey freely admitted in his speech, the germ of the concept came chiefly from Peter Hall, an urban planning expert at Reading University and a former chairman of the Fabian Society, the intellectual center of democratic socialism in Britain.

Ideas do not tend to cross party lines with ease in Britain, and so the fact that a Conservative politician praised a socialist academic as providing the foundation for his proposal is somewhat remarkable in itself. On the other hand, as we shall see, Hall's urban policy suggestions did seem to be more at home on the right of the political spectrum than on the left.

Hall outlined his ideas on dealing with the plight of declining cities in June 1977, in the context of a concept he called the "Freeport."[1] He argued that the extreme problems faced by many British and American cities were actually symptomatic of a structural decline in the traditional industrial economy. Large-scale technological organizations have overshadowed small-scale enterprises, he maintained, leading to fundamental changes in the

95

demand for labor and the location of companies. In addition, manufacturing is giving way to service, governmental, recreational and similar industries, within a business climate where the regulatory bureaucracy has "run amok." The Marxists and Galbraithians may well have a point, Hall suggested, when they claim that the "planned sector" (i.e., government bureaucracy and the big corporations) has effectively stifled the "market sector" that challenged its power.

The critical problem for cities in particular, Hall argued, is that we have managed to kill off much of the innovative entrepreneurship that was once the most important economic feature of central metropolitan areas. Only part of the age-old process is now taking place. Firms are still dying in the cities, or growing larger and moving to other areas. But the most crucial part of the process has all but ceased: People are not filling the gaps as they once did—they are not taking the risk of starting small new businesses.

Hall suggested a number of ways of stimulating the creation of new, job-creating enterprises in cities that still retain some semblance of vitality. Science-based industries might be encouraged to develop around urban universities and in industrial parks. Banking, insurance, entertainment, education, and similar industries might be sought by cities. Tourism might be particularly appropriate as an industry that could be developed consciously by a city.

But, conceded Hall, some cities may have decayed too much for such a recipe to be effective, and a more radical approach may be necessary. "If we really want to help the inner cities, and cities generally, we have to use highly unorthodox methods." Hall believes that the residents of many inner city neighborhoods appear to have been left stranded by the rapid evolution of the advanced postindustrial economy. Their skills, or rather lack of skills, makes them inappropriate for the new high-technology industries, and it is difficult, if not impossible, to train them to the standards necessary—even if we could persuade the companies to locate in the cities:

> Therefore, the answer might be to accept the fact. It would result in a final recipe, which I would call the *Freeport* solution. This is essentially an essay in non-plan. Small, selected areas of inner cities would be simply thrown open to all kinds of initiative, with

96

minimal control. In other words, we would aim to recreate the Hong Kong of the 1950s and 1960s inside inner Liverpool or inner Glasgow.

The radical Freeport plan of Peter Hall would have three central elements.

1. The areas would be outside British foreign exchange and customs controls, as an encouragement to entrepreneurship and overseas capital. Overseas companies and businessmen would be welcome, and all goods could be imported and sold free of tax within the Freeport area—or reexported. Areas of this type, known as free trade zones or foreign trade zones, already exist around the world—Hong Kong, Taiwan, and the Canary Islands are well-known examples. The Freeport version would be "right in the heart of one of our cities."

2. The areas would be "based on fairly shameless free enterprise." Personal and corporate taxation, together with government regulation, would be reduced to the absolute minimum, and the normal range of social services would not be provided. Unions would be allowed within the Freeport, as in Hong Kong, but closed shops would not be permitted. Wage and price guidelines would not apply.

3. Residence in the areas "would be based on choice." Those who chose to live in the Freeport would have to accept the reduced level of benefits along with the reduced level of taxation. For all intents and purposes, the areas would be outside the normal boundaries of the host country, and administered as a Crown Colony or Protectorate—like the relationship of Hong Kong to Britain.

Such a Freeport, admitted Hall, would be a dramatic departure from the pattern of the British welfare state. But it would be an economically vigorous area, where job opportunities for low-skilled and unskilled people would expand rapidly. Hall cautioned, however, that such a bold concept was suitable only for certain locations. "...Since it would represent an extremely drastic last-ditch solution to urban problems, it could be tried only on a very small scale. It is most appropriate to inner city areas that are largely abandoned and denuded of people, or alternatively areas with very grave social and economic problems."

97

Professor Hall was practical enough to accept that it was unlikely that the British government would "act on this suggestion immediately." Given the fact that the socialist Labour Party was in power at the time, this was something of an understatement. But, Hall went on, he was not offering the Freeport as the solution to the country's entire urban problem: It was appropriate only for the areas of greatest distress.

It is hardly surprising that Peter Hall's swashbuckling Freeport idea had a great deal more appeal for conservative politicians than for socialists. Yet even the Conservative Party was hesitant at the thought of creating islands of laissez-faire in the middle of Britain's cities. When Hall met with Sir Geoffrey Howe, who had expressed great interest in the Freeport speech, he found the Conservative spokesman a good deal less inclined than himself to gamble on unfettered capitalism.

There was one aspect of the Freeport concept that did catch the imagination of many Conservatives, however. In his speech, Hall had laid great stress on the need to find new foundations on which to build the "postindustrial" economy—in addition to the more immediate needs of the inner cities. The Freeport would be a mechanism for continuous, unplanned experimentation and adaption. Small entrepreneurs would try out ideas in the area. The good ideas would be an example for others to follow, and the bad ideas would fail. This "test-tube" experimentation might provide a guide to the direction in which the entire economy should move. But a number of people saw even more potential in the laboratory conditions of the Freeport. Perhaps some very basic political and economic questions could be examined under the microscope. We would have the opportunity, they suggested, of comparing the existing structure of government and the economic system with quite radical alternatives, in order to see which really would achieve our goals most effectively. Rather than argue the merits of different systems in the universities and in Parliament, the Freeport might offer a location where theory could be put to the test.

This theme was given its first public airing, a few months after Peter Hall's speech, at a conference organized in London by the Adam Smith Institute. One of the speakers at the conference was Sir Keith Joseph, chief spokesman on industrial matters for the Conservatives, and generally considered to be the party's chief theoretician. In answer to a question, Sir Keith revealed that the

Conservatives were contemplating a set piece contest between the tenets of free enterprise and the planning doctrines of the Labour Party. The next Conservative government, he announced, would set up a series of "Demonstration Zones" within the most depressed parts of the nation's cities, in which government would be virtually dismantled in order to see just what the unfettered market could achieve.

Within these zones, declared Sir Keith, "the Queen's writ shall not run!" Government would be cut to the bone: Taxes would be slashed or eliminated, zoning removed, government monopolies would be ended, and services would be reduced. In short, a "no-government" zone would be created. Since every weapon in the arsenal of government planning had been applied to the blighted inner city, without success, private enterprise was to be given the chance to tackle the problem, and the country would be able to see which did the better job. Planning and un-planning would meet in combat, like medieval champions at the joust.

The considered ideas of senior Conservatives on the demonstration area were eventually laid out in a major speech by Sir Geoffrey Howe in the summer of 1978.[2] It was in this speech, delivered in the Isle of Dogs in London's depressed dockland, that Sir Geoffrey outlined for the first time his proposal for the creation of inner-city "Enterprise Zones."

"Two distinct philosophies are on offer," said Sir Geoffrey. On the one hand there was the system of bureaucratic planning that had resulted only in overregulation and economic stagnation. He saw this system as primarily responsible for the economic and social problems afflicting the cities. In contrast, he said, there was the system offered by the Conservatives, based on "private initiative, widely dispersed and properly rewarded."

The legacy of government planning, he went on, could be seen most clearly in the major cities. Great expanses of land lay unused, either owned by the government or ensnared in government red tape. Elsewhere, whole sections of cities "continue to crumble in the name of housing action areas and the like," while countless expensive programs seemed only to expand the bureaucracy, not employment or housing.

The situation in some neighborhoods was so bad, in Sir Geoffrey's view, that the urban policies currently under discussion could not conceivably produce any significant results. There seemed to be only two possible conclusions: "Some might argue that they are beyond help and would abandon them as inner city ghost-towns—a doleful monument to our collective incompetence." But Sir Geoffrey discounted this as feckless and inhumane. The alternative option was to appreciate that these depressed areas actually have some very real advantages. They are often close to thriving commercial areas, and to harbors or other commercial gateways. In many cases, the land had already been cleared and could be developed. "And they still have communities who cherish a sense of civic pride but yearn for jobs, real jobs—who are looking for a window of hope for the future." Such people, he said, have shown a remarkable ability to hang on, and to create some opportunities, "in the teeth of institutional inertia."

Rather than write these areas off, therefore:

Can we, if we have the courage and imagination, transform them into our greatest opportunities? Are we perhaps driven to the conclusion that the remedies that need to be applied generally should be even more dramatically applied in the most afflicted areas?

...The original prosperity of our cities was founded on the pursuit of profit. Why should we not again seek a solution that is based on the view that those who help restore prosperity are entitled to expect financial reward—and on a substantial scale?

Reminding his audience of Peter Hall's Freeport idea, Sir Geoffrey noted that Hong Kong, Singapore, and smaller free trade zones such as Shannon in the Irish Republic, provided a clear lesson that remarkable economic activity can occur in the most unlikely and seemingly inhospitable locations, providing taxes, customs, and unnecessary regulations are significantly reduced. But he agreed with Hall that the Freeport concept was indeed a drastic last-ditch solution. He felt that he could not support quite such a dramatic experiment, particularly as there was the danger that the Freeport could become a tax haven for "every individual citizen and footloose company office." Nevertheless, he did see the Freeport as a valuable "yardstick against which to judge more modest proposals."

Howe's more modest proposal—the Enterprise Zone—differed in some important ways from Hall's concept, even though there were some close similarities in the underlying philosophy and the policies that would be applied. While Sir Geoffrey saw the zones as distinct from other measures that should be adopted throughout the country, he, like Hall, saw the zones as radical versions of a climate that should be created throughout the country to stimulate economic activity. "The idea would be to set up test market areas or laboratories in which to enable fresh policies to prime the pump of prosperity, and to establish their potential for doing so elsewhere."

In addition, the zones would offer a real chance for people of differing viewpoints to put their ideas to the test, and provide the opportunity for a genuine confrontation between free enterprise and the planned society:

> My proposals are not intended to be a politically exclusive idea but an experiment that could fire the imagination of people of all parties or in none. I believe that it would be worthwhile ensuring that part of any Enterprise Zone could be available to non-commercial groups who wished, for example, to establish experimental workers' cooperatives.... If the Tribune Group[3] or the Socialist Workers' Party wanted part of an Enterprise Zone to themselves—well, why not?

Sir Geoffrey proposed the establishment of four or five such zones in the first instance, in locations that had substantial tracts of urban land that could be developed quickly, in order to make profits and create jobs. The main features of the zones, he said, should be the following:

1. Detailed planning controls would cease to apply. Providing a building was for a legal purpose, complied with the most basic antipollution, health and safety standards, and met stated height and similar restrictions, it would be allowed automatically.
2. Local and national governments would be required to dispose of any land they owned in the zone within a specified time, by auction to private bidders.
3. All new developments in the zone would be free of rent control.
4. Entrepreneurs who established enterprises in the zone would be exempt from Development Land Tax (i.e., capital gains resulting from development). In addition, there would be a

reduction, or even an elimination, of rates (i.e., property taxes) on all business premises.

5. Businesses would be given a guarantee that the tax laws would not be changed to their disadvantage for at least a stated period. On the other hand, no government grants or subsidies would be available to any enterprise in the zone.

6. Certain other legal obligations would not apply, such as wage and price controls and certain (unspecified) provisions of the Employment Protection Act.[4]

7. All the conditions would be guaranteed for a stated "and substantial" number of years.

The effect of these changes within the Enterprise Zones, according to Howe, would be to offer people the *chance* to take risks and make money, and thereby create employment and general prosperity. Nothing would be underwritten, but the obstacles to success would be removed. And the same would be true for the inner cities as for the entrepreneurs. "No one can be sure whether my suggested approach would work or not....But it is about time we were prepared to make some fresh starts."

Sir Geoffrey seemed to harbor few illusions about the difficulties of turning ideas into legislative reality. He knew there were "grey men" whose job it is to consider the "administrative difficulties" of anything novel and to start "manufacturing the small print" that would kill the initiative. Such opposition would arise and would have to be met head-on.

Notwithstanding such bureaucratic foot-dragging, Howe conceded, the question of how an Enterprise Zone should be administered did pose some problems, especially as some potential sites would probably fall under the jurisdiction of more than one local government. In order that the zones should not become hopelessly embroiled in disputes between competing authorities, he suggested that a new authority should be created specifically for the zones "to be available as a kind of standard kit for those communities that wished to apply for it." The essential purpose of such an authority would be to dispose of property for economic development. To ensure that the residents of the zone would gain some direct benefits from this, they should perhaps be given an equity stake in the authority, or have the right to require it to buy their property if they did not choose to remain in the zone.

The Idea Takes Shape

Sir Geoffrey Howe's speech aroused considerable intellectual interest, but the general reaction was restrained. It was, after all, only a personal idea put forward by one—albeit very senior—opposition politician. It was not official Conservative policy, and there was every reason to believe that the Conservatives would be in opposition for some time to come. So there seemed little prospect of the Enterprise Zone concept becoming reality in the near future, if ever. The Enterprise Zone was seen by most of the press as simply an example of "kite-flying" (as the London *Financial Times* put it)—quite normal for a party in opposition but a poor guide to future policy. Nevertheless the *Financial Times* did take the opportunity to amuse its readers by speculating on the street names that might be seen in an Enterprise Zone of the future. Columnist Peter Riddell imagined that they might be named after "heroes of the cause": possibly "Hayek Boulevard and Thatcher Plaza."[5]

When the Labour government collapsed unexpectedly early in 1979, and Mrs. Thatcher's Conservatives were swept to power, the Enterprise Zone ceased to be merely an idea. In his budget statement of March 1980 the new Chancellor of the Exchequer (i.e., Treasury Secretary) Sir Geoffrey Howe announced that the government intended to set up some six zones, each of approximately 500 acres. In the official policy statement that accompanied the budget announcement, the details of the zones were made clear. The strong party system that is an essential feature of British parliamentary democracy ensures that a government's proposals are rarely altered drastically during the legislative process, and so the final legislation creating the Enterprise Zones differed little from the original proposals in the budget. There was no "Enterprise Zone Act" as such. Instead, the changes were incorporated into two "standard" government bills—the Local Government Planning and Land Act, and the Finance Act. These measures were finally passed into law in November 1980.

The provisions of the Enterprise Zone legislation in Britain fall into four broad categories. There are provisions which deal with the designation and administration of the zones; tax changes; modifications of planning and zoning procedures within the zones; and a smaller number of special regulatory changes.

103

1. Designation and Administration

The secretary of state for the Department of the Environment (which is responsible for urban policy) is empowered to *invite* a local authority to submit proposals for an Enterprise Zone. This local authority would normally be the city government, but it could be another element of local government or a development corporation. The final right of designation rests with the secretary, but he cannot designate an area as a zone if the local authority does not accept the invitation. The suggested zone must be made public before the decision is made, so that objections can be heard and modifications made.

In designating an area an Enterprise Zone, the fiscal concessions provided by the central government come into effect, but only after there has been an agreement between the national government and the local authority on a proposal for the substantial relaxation of development planning procedures within the zone.

Before the fiscal concessions come into play, there must also be agreement on the boundaries of the zone. When there has been agreement on both the boundaries and the planning regime, the body that was invited to submit proposals becomes the "Enterprise Zone Authority," charged with the administration of the zone.

The designation will last for an agreed period, usually 10 years. During that period, the secretary of state has no power to withdraw the designation.

The nature of the development planning regime within the zone can be modified in the face of demand or experience, but this requires the agreement of both the Secretary of State and the Enterprise Zone Authority. The Secretary does have the unilateral power, however, to make certain technical changes and to extend the life of the zone. But he cannot reduce the time span, or alter the boundaries, without the consent of the Enterprise Zone Authority.

104

2. Tax Changes

Development Land Tax

Development value realized from the disposal of land in an Enterprise Zone within 10 years of the zone's designation is exempt from the tax (a capital gains tax). Normally, this would be levied at a rate of 60%.

Rates (Property Tax)

Industrial, commercial, and retailing property is exempt from all property tax. This does not apply to residential buildings, however. In the case of mixed use structures, property taxes are payable on the residential element. The local authority will be reimbursed by the national Treasury for all the lost revenue, on both existing buildings and new development.

Capital (Depreciation) Allowances

Even before the Enterprise Zone legislation, there was an immediate allowance against corporation or income tax of 50% of capital expenditures for the construction, extension, or improvement of *industrial* buildings, with a 4% annual writing down allowance thereafter. For *hotels*, the initial allowance was 20%. No such allowances were available for offices, shops, or other commercial buildings. Plant and machinery was given a 100% allowance in the year the expenditure was incurred.

The Enterprise Zone legislation removed these distinctions and increased the allowance on buildings to 100% in the first year for all zone businesses. The business may choose to take a smaller initial allowance and write off the remainder at 25% per year. If the building is sold within 25 years of the expenditure, however, a balancing charge, or clawback, comes into force. The allowance applies both to expenditures made within the life of the zone and to expenditures arising from a contract made during the zone's existence.

3. Planning Simplification

Obtaining permission to build or make modifications to existing buildings can be a lengthy, expensive, and complicated process in Britain. In addition to broad zoning restrictions, applications must be made to the local council planning committee. Detailed plans must be submitted, and the committee can require minute changes in the plans before permission is given to build.

Within an Enterprise Zone, this time-consuming procedure is streamlined. The proposal for a zone put forward by a local authority and agreed to by the secretary of state must contain broad zoning conditions. Any development plan that complies with these conditions will be given automatic clearance—that is, the authority cannot delay it or require modifications. If the proposed development does not meet the conditions it may still go ahead, but it would have to go through the procedure of obtaining planning permission in the normal manner. The simplified procedure for permission must include the enforcement of controls over hazardous or polluting developments, and the usual safety and health requirements.

Even if a development meets the broad, streamlined standards applicable to the zone, special permission will still be needed from the Enterprise Zone Authority for any element of a building plan that is considered a "reserved matter" under the terms of the Enterprise Zone agreement. These might include the design of access points to the highway where there were safety implications and similar technical matters, but they could not include major parts of a development.

Once permission to build has been given in the zone, either through the automatic or the discretionary procedures, the developer is be free to go ahead with the plan at any time during the life of the zone, even if the conditions of the Enterprise Zone have been modified in the interim.

4. Simplication of Regulation

Statistical Information

Although the details of the cutback in statistical information required by the government have not yet been made clear, it is intended that the paperwork demanded from zone businesses for government purposes will be kept "to a bare minimum." The only item actually contained in the legislation dealt with industrial training boards. This is an employee training program under which a levy is imposed on employers, and information is required from them. In return, training-related grants are available. In an Enterprise Zone, a firm may opt out of the entire scheme.

Customs Facilities

Applications for "inward processing relief" will be given priority if the applicant is an Enterprise Zone firm. This is an arrangement by which goods imported for processing and subsequent reexport outside the European Community are not liable for customs charges. This does not constitute a new concession, but the priority given to applications should make the zones more attractive to processing companies. In addition, the conditions applying to private customs warehouses are relaxed within Enterprise Zones.

The Measures in Summary

The package of changes contained in the British Enterprise Zone legislation are calculated to achieve a particular effect in the chosen locations. It is very important to distinguish between those intended results and the broad ideas put forward earlier by Sir Geoffrey and others, and it is particularly important, when comparing the legislation with the theoretical discussion, to appreciate the importance of what was *not* in the measures passed by Parliament.

The provisions of the legislation make it very clear that the primary aim of Britain's Enterprise Zones is to encourage industrial and commercial redevelopment in derelict or cleared areas of cities. It is not the purpose of the zones to bring about the mixed use of existing buildings, or to stimulate the housing market within the zones. Nor, for that matter, does the aim seem to be to encourage small new enterprises. The principal goal appears to be *new construction* and the establishment of branches by medium-sized and larger corporations. As we shall see, the choice of sites announced so far serves to confirm this impression.

The exemption of businesses from Development Land Tax, together with the 100% capital allowance for business-related buildings, will provide a powerful incentive for new construction or expansions undertaken by tax-paying companies. The capital allowance is particularly attractive to retailing and commercial companies, who are not eligible for the 50% allowance available everywhere for industrial concerns. The 100% abatement of property taxes on business premises further increases the attractiveness of property development within the zones.

The British zones are not geared toward depressed residential neighborhoods. The target is the old industrial slums and urban wastelands of the major cities: Victorian factories that closed down years ago, the empty warehouses and silent wharves of now-obsolete dockland districts, and the great expanses of government-owned land that are so common in Britain's major cities. The assumption is that by encouraging companies to develop these sites, a boost will be given to the entire local economy, leading to jobs and opportunities for the nearby residents.

There are some very important elements of Sir Geoffrey's first speech on the Enterprise Zone that are absent from the legislative package creating the zones. Some cynics might even argue that the "grey men" that the chancellor feared would put small print into the measure have actually succeeded in taking the large print out!

There is nothing in the legislation to *require* the selling of government-owned land in the zones. In most of the sites actually chosen so far, a large proportion of the land is owned directly by government or by nationalized industries. So there is still considerable scope for the government to regulate activity within many of the zones. In addition, new residential property in the zones will not be free of rent controls, nor will they be free of property tax, nor will they enjoy the capital allowances available to other buildings. The Enterprise Zones will therefore hold little attraction as sites for housing improvements or new construction. The unstated but very evident strategy is to make the segregation of residential and business land uses even more pronounced in the inner cities. There is little chance of the diversity considered so essential by Jane Jacobs ever becoming a feature of the British Enterprise Zones.

One also looks in vain for any significant reduction in business regulation in the legislation, other than the simplified planning procedures for new construction. There is nothing in the package which will reduce the constricting impact of the employment-related legislation so widely criticized by the business community. The government is evidently prepared to go no further in the zones than it is for the country as a whole.

The alteration in the customs and warehousing procedures may seem to be a step forward from the original Howe plan, but it is only a small step forward. The changes do not constitute the mechanism for a free trade zone, and are certainly not the basis for a Freeport of the Hall variety. In defense of the limited trade concessions, government officials have pointed out that Britain's membership in the European Economic Community imposes severe restrictions on the freedom to establish free trade areas.

Noticeably absent from the legislation is any explicit commitment to the idea of social experimentation and "laboratory" testing of political ideas that was such an interesting feature of Sir Geoffrey's original concept. It is always possible that part of an Enterprise Zone may be set aside as a site for radical innovations such as workers' cooperatives or even libertarian communities, but the tone of the measures suggest that this is unlikely. Rapid industrial and commercial development seems to be the first and only order of business—there is little room left for inventive approaches aimed at strengthening urban neighborhoods.

The British Enterprise Zones seem only indirectly concerned with new entrepreneurs. There are very few incentives designed to encourage anyone with limited means to save hard and take the risk of setting up in an Enterprise Zone. The provisions seem suited exclusively to the businessman with plenty of capital and a heavy tax bill, who is in a position to hire a bulldozer and put his money into property. Although this may lead to factories becoming available to some smaller, growing firms, there is little to help the man with a bright idea who needs an old garage, or a basement, or some other inexpensive place where he can start.

The British Enterprise Zones may well provide incentives for already-established companies to put their new facilities into depressed areas, or even to close down existing plants and move to the zones. They might well lead to location decisions that are very beneficial to the areas chosen as sites. But there is little reason to suppose that they will throw open the door to new entrepreneurs who might be able to create the jobs needed in poor neighborhoods and who would add to the fabric of the whole economy. There is little prospect of any Hong Kongs in Britain's inner cities.

The legislative package placed before Parliament and later passed was certainly less sweeping than the tone of Sir Geoffrey's original speech. Apparently there was some dismay among Conservative councillors who attended a local government conference where the package was outlined just a few weeks before it was announced in Parliament. Some councillors argued that the early idea of full-blooded capitalism in the inner cities had been so watered down as to be worse than useless. It seems that the original Howe plan had languished in the hands of the "grey men" of the civil service for nearly a year, and that it had to be given to a committee of hard-line ministers to see what could be salvaged. If one compares the fine print of Sir Geoffrey's proposal with the provisions of the legislation one could conclude that the salvaging job had been reasonably successful. But if one compares the thrust of the measures with the bold image created in 1978, it is difficult not to agree with one critic who suggested that "after much labor, the mountain brought forth its mouse."[6]

Although strong reservations about the Enterprise Zones have come from many Conservative politicians and academics, there was no lack of enthusiasm among local councils. When the Enterprise Zone proposal was presented to Parliament in March 1980, the government announced that it would approach six or seven local authorities and invite them to submit applications for sites of approximately 500 acres "in an area of physical and economic decay where conventional government policies have not succeeded in generating self-sustaining economic activity."[7] The government announced that certain cities were already on the short list for consideration: Glasgow in Scotland, Belfast in Northern Ireland, Swansea in Wales, and five English cities.

Despite the fairly precise locations that the government seemed to be considering, it received twenty-five applications over the next few months from councils wishing to be considered. Six alone came from metropolitan London. The overwhelming majority of applications came from cities controlled by the opposition Labour Party—to the undisguised amusement of Conservatives and the embarrassment of senior Labour officials. By the end of July seven sites had been chosen, subject to successful agreements concerning the boundaries, zoning and building permission, and the administrative arrangement in each case. Two more sites were announced in October, and a further two in February 1981.

The geographic spread of the cities reflected both economic and political considerations. Northern Ireland has been awarded one site in West Belfast; Scotland has so far received one in the depressed Clydebank area; and Wales a site in Swansea. The declining northern cities of England have been well represented with five sites, including one in the old port city of Liverpool, a location in nearby Manchester, and one in Newcastle. Two sites have been chosen in distressed parts of the formerly very prosperous Midlands, one of which is in Corby, a former "new" town that became a problem area with the closure of a steel plant, the town's principal employer. The only site, so far, in the south of England is in the dockland district of London's East End. The location, the Isle of Dogs, is where Sir Geoffrey Howe first introduced the Enterprise Zone concept. The average size of the sites is about 500 acres, but there is a wide range. The Belfast zone, for example, covers only 200 acres. The Newcastle site, in contrast, is 1,150 acres in size.

It is quite clear from the nature of most of the sites that the aim is major redevelopment. Virtually all the locations chosen are totally derelict, or else they contain large, vacant industrial buildings. Generally the government or a nationalized industry owns most of the site. The zone in Liverpool, for instance, includes within its boundaries two large but empty factories, one of which is the government-owned British Leyland Corporation, together with a part of a disused former municipal airport. In its initial discussions with the Liverpool council, the central government made it very clear that the final boundaries should give priorities to areas which contained vacant buildings and land immediately available for development.[8] Almost half of the Manchester site consists of a disused section of Salford's municipal docks, and most of the Isle of Dogs location consists of redundant docks and dockland buildings owned by the city.

This mixture of large vacant buildings and open land, much of it owned by government, is common to almost all the sites chosen so far. They are generally derelict heavy industrial centers or dock facilities close to the downtown metropolitan area. While they tend

111

to be close to low-income housing districts, they are practically unpopulated.

Because the British zones require significant redevelopment of old industrial land it is expected that considerable reclamation and infrastructure work will be necessary in many of the locations. In the Swansea site in Wales a great deal of work has already been completed, including the removal of slag heaps and the installation of roads, sewers, power lines, and water pipes. But several million pounds will still need to be spent to provide basic structural services and to remove toxic waste material. Similar expenditures will be needed in many of the sites where unusable industrial buildings dominate the zone. In some other locations, however, the basic requirements already exist and development will be possible almost immediately.

Reactions to the Zones

Despite the belief in some Conservative circles that the Enterprise Zone package was a pale shadow of what had been promised, the initial press reaction to the measures was generally enthusiastic. The right-leaning London *Daily Telegraph*, in an editorial entitled "Green Light Districts," saw the whole proposal as "a deeply attractive idea. There are skills and ambitions waiting to turn a couple of huts and a work bench into a growth point." Using the words of one entrepreneur, the newspaper went on to remind its readers that "inside every moonlighter there's a small businessman trying to get out."[9]

The Economist saw the plan as "wholly admirable," but also sounded a few words of caution. All local councils, the journal pointed out, hate to give up power. Left-wing councils especially could be expected to resent strongly "the government's swash-buckling capitalist intentions." Sabotage could therefore be expected—probably by councils trying to extend the scope of the "reserved matters" over which they were to retain control. Moreover, said *The Economist*, there was the distinct danger that the Enterprise Zones would not create any new jobs at all, but merely lure already-successful companies out of more attractive parts of a city. The journal also predicted understandable opposition from firms just outside the zones who feared subsidized

112

competition. "There's no escape from that one," it concluded, "unless the whole country becomes an Enterprise Zone."[10]

The reaction to the Conservative proposals from the opposition Labour Party and its supporters was as negative as one might expect. The philosophical divide between the parties in Britain is much deeper than in the United States, and it is rare for the party out of power to be supportive of any government measure, particularly when it is seen as a challenge to the opposition's whole approach. So it was hardly surprising that the free enterprise, antiplanning theme of the Enterprise Zone provoked little short of apoplexy among several Labour members of Parliament. Frank Hooley, for example, maintained that instead of producing employment for local people, the zones would "create jobs for property sharks, real estate men, lawyers, accountants and tax fiddlers." Speculation would be rife, he claimed, and "any potty scheme" would be able to benefit from the incentives offered.[11] Other Labour MPs believed that the zones would attract the worst sort of businesses out of the woodwork, such as scrap metal dealers, used car sellers and sex shop—"possibly the only imaginable development which could be worse that the derelict sites themselves" according to one Labour member.[12]

The Trades Union Congress, Britain's AFL-CIO, detected what it felt to be a direct threat to the entire labor movement. "Rogue employers" would be drawn to these areas, it predicted—just the kind of firm that would be most likely to "undermine and weaken the rights of workers, especially in relation to unfair dismissal and union recognition."[13] The left-dominated National Executive of the Labour Party (NEC) was extremely irritated that so many Labour-controlled city councils had almost fallen over themselves to submit applications for Enterprise Zones. The zones were simply an insidious plot, announced the NEC, to reproduce the "horrors" of Hong Kong, Singapore and Chile in Britain's cities (Chile was presumably added in case the other two did not seem sufficiently horrific to Labour councillors). The social and political environment of these and other places "where Milton Friedman's theories hold sway" was deemed to be "completely unacceptable to a modern democracy." The Enterprise Zones, argued the NEC, would be the new "industrial slums" of the 1980s, with bad designs and poor environments that the local communities would have to endure for years.

113

The NEC's strongest objections, however, centered on what it saw as the dark purpose behind the Enterprise Zone. The "myth" that the zones were intended as a positive response to the problems of the inner city should be laid to rest, it said, and those flirting with the concept should realize that

> it is really aimed at winning the political arguments for market rather than planning solutions, for private rather than public enterprise. It forms part of the Tory strategy for weakening the power of organised labor. As such, the idea of Enterprise Zones as a bi-partisan venture supported by the Labour Party has to be rejected.[14]

Apparently, the Labour Party felt that it was not yet ready to take part in a test between market and socialist solutions to the problems of the city.

Politicians and officials at the local level have generally ignored the philosophical issues surrounding the Enterprise Zone, and have concentrated on the purely economic potential of the idea. The general feeling among councils applying for sites seems to be that the zones offer a chance to stimulate employment not just in the immediate vicinity, but throughout the region in which they are located. Evan Lewis, leader of the Swansea City Council, for example, sees the Enterprise Zone as adding considerable weight to the council's broad range of economic policies for the area. Provost Jim McKendrick, leader of the Clydebank council, took a similar view when the Scottish site was announced. The Enterprise Zone would be a "blood transfusion," he said, which would provide a boost to the entire Glasgow economy.[15]

Although the choice of sites by the government was only the prelude to detailed discussions with the local authorities regarding the boundaries and other features of the zones, there has been strong interest in many of the sites by the business community. Within twenty-four hours of the announcement of the Dudley site, for instance, more than thirty inquiries had been received by the city council.[16] A month leater the council said that more than two hundred companies had shown interest.[17]

There is, of course, a realm of difference between the expression of interest and a commitment. None of the zones were to be operational until the summer of 1981. So it is impossible as yet to determine what kinds of businesses will locate in the zones, or what the net impact will be. Nevertheless, strong concerns have been voiced by many people who feel that although a great deal of activity may result, thanks to the incentives given, it may lead to quite different results from those expected by the government or the cities concerned.

There is a particular fear that the zones may have a detrimental effect on nearby areas, rather than contribute to their improvement. The Clydebank location, for instance, is close to a downtown shopping complex in which the city has a $25-million investment. The one-year-100% building depreciation allowance given to zone firms makes the Enterprise Zone very attractive to retailers, who are not eligible for the 50% allowance available generally to industrial firms. This allowance, combined with abatement of property taxes, and the fact that crime is not a significant problem in the location, has caused many to worry that the zone could just become a magnet for large retail outlets. The zone might thereby become a major competitor with the downtown shopping district for the same income stream. In an attempt to deal with this possibility, the council has been pressing the government to agree to a zoning plan for the site that would limit the level of retailing that would be permitted.

Other councils have faced the same problem. A new shopping center recently opened in Swansea, and there is great concern in the city that if large retailers move into the Enterprise Zone there would be a threat to jobs and investment in the city center. The issue is particularly sensitive in the Manchester site, since a major hypermarket chain was already applying for planning permission to build on a 24-acre lot within the site when it was announced. If allowed, the hypermarket would have been the second largest in Britain, and the property tax and other allowances would have given it a considerable commercial advantage over other shopping centers in the area.

By agreeing to the site as an Enterprise Zone, the Manchester council was faced with the dilemma of possibly having to give automatic approval to the hypermarket development as part of the zoning agreement with the government, or losing the chance for an Enterprise Zone in what is considered the prime location. The government was understandably reluctant to make concessions, however, because the freedom to develop with the minimum of planning controls is central to the idea of the Enterprise Zone. But after strong representations by the city it was agreed that a size restriction would apply to retailers in the Manchester zone.

The wrangles over large retailing in the zones is a good example of the tension between the central and local governments foreseen by *The Economist*. Although cities are always quite happy to accept financial concessions for businesses that locate in their area, and to receive a reimbursement from the national Treasury for abated property taxes, there always remains the desire to hold onto the development planning reins. A concession over one aspect of business in even one zone is an important breach in the principle that development within the zones should be a product of market forces, and not of a city plan. Despite the strength of the arguments for it, the concession will make it all the more difficult to resist other special cases.

It has been suggested by some commentators, such as Judy Hillman of the London *Observer*, that the government made a tactical blunder in naming the chosen locations before detailed negotiations with the local authorities had been completed. "Before the choice of zones was made," Hillman wrote, "competition was so keen that Whitehall (i.e., central government) officials were simply telling councils that they could either accept the largely laissez-faire terms as they stood or drop out of the running. Now the local authorities will no longer be frightened to press for the terms they want."[18]

The government did, indeed, put itself into a political corner by naming areas where agreement had been reached only in principle, not in detail. It would be very difficult for the government to withdraw the invitation to propose a zone once that invitation has been made public. So the announcements have strengthened the bargaining position of the chosen cities—at the expense of the central government. But it is hard to see how this could be avoided. The government could hardly have conducted very complex negotiations over the details of sites without giving some assurance that the site would be chosen if agreement were reached. This would not only have been an enormous waste of time, but it could have raised false hopes. While the uncertainty continued, it could also have been very damaging to local investment patterns and invited speculation.

The hypermarket issue is less of an illustration of the predictable contest between local planners and the government, however, than it is a necessary result of the basic financial incentives in the British package. When one provides incentives aimed at large industrial, commercial and retailing corporations, one should not be too surprised if large corporations react to them. The large retailing sector received the greatest benefits under the legislation, compared with the normal allowances the sector receives; therefore, large retailers are naturally very interested in the zones. Problems of this kind necessarily follow when redevelopment and job-creation are based on large corporations rather than on the small-business sector.

A related fear expressed by many people in Britain is that the Enterprise Zones as now constituted may not only pose a threat for nearby business centers in the city but may also be potentially disastrous for adjacent areas not lucky enough to be included within the boundary. Borders have to be somewhere, and somebody is going to be on the wrong side of them. According to the critics, the investment and business prospects for these firms is going to be very bleak.

It is too early yet to gauge the strength of this argument. Many proponents of the zones argue that the long run effect may be precisely the opposite: that the boost given by the zones will cause increased investment in the whole area. But there is no doubt that the anxiety felt by border firms is very real. In the Swansea zone, the border was even redrawn to include some new factories built for let. The owner was convinced that exclusion from the zone would have spelled disaster: "We were horrified when we learned that our factories were just outside the 350 acre zone. Unless we could persuade the government to change their minds we knew we would never dispose of the factories because the conditions at the Enterprise Zone are so favorable."[19]

Opposition from local businesses not included in the zone has been very strong in Dudley, in the West Midlands. Within a month of the announcement that a site had been chosen, more than 200 local small-businessmen had joined together to launch a campaign against the zone. Claiming that 5,000 jobs could be in jeopardy, leaders of the campaign cited the property tax relief as the main cause of their anger. According to spokesmen for the campaign, firms in the zone would be able to use property tax relief to cut

117

prices. Some existing firms in the zone, they claimed, could save as much as £100,000 a year. The campaign called for a strict vetting procedure of applicant businesses to ensure that there would be no competition with other area businesses, and pressed for property taxes in the zones to be brought up to normal levels within three years.[20]

The antizone lobby in Dudley has not been without its own critics. Describing the whole business protest as "zone moans," one local newspaper suggested that some of the firms taking part in the campaign could use a little competition to wake them up. They were not so much against competition from an Enterprise Zone, the paper argued, but simply competition in principle. Even if the zone were miles away, firms would still be striving for the same general market. "Industries are not like sweet shops, selling to a passing trade."[21]

In fairness to the antizone businessmen, it should be emphasized that their strongest criticisms centered on the benefits that would befall companies already in the zone, rather than on new companies. But this is confined to the property tax exemption. The increased allowances against tax for building expenditures helps only a new firm or one engaged in expansion. Yet even the property tax abatement can mean considerable immediate savings for existing firms. In Dudley, there are about fifty companies already located in the zone site, and these will be exempt from property taxes for at least ten years. Savings for individual firms can be quite considerable. In the Swansea zone, for example, one factory belonging to the Morgan Crucible group will have its property tax bill reduced by nearly half a million dollars a year.[22]

If a property tax exemption benefits firms that do not expand and generate new jobs, one might question its inclusion in the package. But government officials suggest that the "windfall" to existing firms is actually quite small in total, compared with the benefits to new companies, and that to try to distinguish between new and old firms is administratively very difficult. In any case, one might argue, it would be unfair to give all the benefits to the newcomers, and deny them to those firms that have hung on in a depressed area. In addition, say officials, the property tax exemption is particularly helpful to new and small firms, which may have little or no profit against which they can apply allowances, but have to pay property taxes.

Yet the government has been influenced by the criticism that existing firms will benefit considerably from the property tax exemption. In determining the boundaries, every attempt has been made to minimize the number of established businesses that would exist in any zone. In several cases, such as in Newcastle and Corby, the result has been that the "zone" is in fact a multi-zone, with small, island-zones close to the primary site.

The debate over the effect of Enterprise Zones on nearby business districts raises the general issue of the possible effects of the zones on the national economy. If prosperity comes to a zone because companies move from elsewhere, or because firms locate new branches in a zone rather than somewhere else simply because of the concessions, then we would be helping one area at the expense of another. Such relocation is bound to occur to some extent. But if it were to become the chief cause of economic improvement in the zones, and there was little or no net addition to the national economy, the zones would be open to very serious criticisms. If all we do is shift jobs around for the benefit of a few chosen areas, we have not helped very much.

The British government is well aware there is a real danger that local growth in the zones may result from relocation. In the debates on the Enterprise Zone, government ministers made it clear that the goal would be to create new enterprises. Tom King, a minister for local government affairs, argued that relocation was not likely to be that great a factor, since a company already established elsewhere would face considerable expense and risk in moving to a zone. He did not feel the zones would have a "vacuum or sucking effect, drawing outside industries straight into an Enterprise Zone." Rather, he said:

> Their prime purpose is not to attract industry from elsewhere. Their first purpose is to encourage and stimulate the creation of new industry and enterprise. One reason for the experiment is to see whether this is the effect and to see what the balance is. We all know that there will be some attraction from elsewhere....Any of these assistance or promotion schemes runs that risk. The question is whether this scheme can also stimulate the growth of new enterprises and that is what interests us particularly.

There is no intention, the minister went on, "to claim credit for our policy merely because we have an oasis of prosperity surrounded by a desert of dereliction, as the result of the Enterprise Zone, to the disadvantage of its surrounding areas." The zones would be monitored very carefully, he pointed out, to distinguish new firms from transfers.[23]

It should be remembered that the Enterprise Zones in Britain are very much an experimental approach. They are small and limited in number. If the overall effect is to cause relocation rather than new creations, then at least the consequences will be confined and we will have learned something. If that does not occur, the zones might be modified, or pronounced an interesting failure. If they do succeed, however, in stimulating new activity, then some important lessons will have been learned for national urban and economic policy.

The greatest danger seen by many strong supporters of the Enterprise Zone *concept*, however, is that the version passed by Parliament may be ineffective, or even detrimental, because it ignores many of the most basic elements of the original idea. If the present version does fail, they fear, it could discredit the whole approach without being a real test of it.

What is particularly troublesome is that many supporters of the concept as such feel that the incentives in the legislation do little to dismantle the barriers facing small entrepreneurs—the front line troops of the Enterprise Zone idea. The small-business sector in Britain is among the weakest in the West. A 1976 study showed that Germany, for instance, has only 10% more people than Britain, but it has 40% more small firms.[24] And it is not just the size of the sector that causes alarm. The small-business sector does not include a healthy proportion of young, innovative companies. The average age of the small sector in Britain is three times that in America. David Birch's work in the United States shows that small, independent firms are essential to job creation in depressed urban areas, and the principal job generating sector in the national economy. Although there is no analysis of Britain's small businesses as sweeping in scope as Birch's, Department of Employment statistics indicate that smaller companies have provided all the growth in manufacturing jobs over the last decade.[25] In Britain, as well as America, small firms are more innovative, more adaptable, and produce more of the jobs needed by inner-city residents.

Despite the proven importance of the small entrepreneur, the incentives in the Enterprise Zones appear to be geared far more, if not exclusively, to the larger corporations. The government argues that the zones will be attractive to all innovative businessmen, and that there will be considerable opportunities for the small entrepreneur. Very large, abandoned factories exist in many of the zones, say officials, and the development allowance should encourage developers to divide some of these into workshops and small factories which will be very suitable to new small firms.

Time will tell if this does happen, but the feeling that the zones offer very little to small companies is quite widespread, despite the government's optimistic words. The Confederation of British Industry (CBI), representing larger companies, has endorsed the Enterprise Zone idea as an experiment that may provide clear evidence that the whole country would benefit from the relaxation of regulation and controls. Yet the CBI sees only:

> limited benefit to smaller firms in the measures. The relief of property taxes, and the simplified planning procedure will be of some assistance, but since most small firms are not owner-occupiers the exemption from Development Land Tax and the increased capital allowances on buildings will have no direct effect.[26]

Similar arguments have been raised by groups representing small companies. The Association of Independent Businesses (AIB), for example, complained in testimony to the government that the planned zones would give considerable encouragement to property developers, but precious little to small traders. "Redevelopment and small business enterprises have proved incompatible in the past," said the AIB, "and there is nothing in these proposals to provide for a more balanced relationship in the future."

The AIB believes that the British zones will offer most scope to the kind of "sophisticated tax planning" that is seen only in larger companies. There is little, on the other hand, in the way of help for new enterprises in their early, often unprofitable years. Like the CBI, the AIB sees no assistance to small companies in the elimination of Development Land Tax, or from the improved capital allowances on buildings, since new, small firms rarely build, and usually lack the profits against which the allowances can be taken for tax purposes. Although the property tax exemption could help small businessmen who own their premises, the AIB sees little benefit for the majority, who rent. The group does not believe the reduction in costs to the landlord will lead to lower rents, since the total fiscal and planning package will boost the value of property. Unless special provisions are somehow added to the existing package, the combined effect of the incentives will not be to encourage new entrepreneurs, but to crowd them out of the zones.[27]

In its suggested amendments to Enterprise Zone measures put before Parliament, the AIB put forward some interesting proposals. They argued, in effect, that the incentives in the zones should be grouped into two catergories. If a concession was being *tested* in the Enterprise Zone, with the aim of general introduction nationally at a later date if it were found useful, then it should run the full ten-year life of the zone. If, on the other hand, the concession had the limited purpose of stimulating development within the zone, it should apply only to the first three years of a company's operation.

This distinction would seem to have some merit. If the idea is indeed to give an area a "shot in the arm," then that is what companies should receive, rather than be put on a respirator for ten years. There is a real danger that the Enterprise Zones will attract some very marginal companies that can survive only with substantial tax concessions. If such companies cannot make it over the start-up hurdle within three years, then there is a lot to be said for switching off the life support and allowing them to be replaced by others willing to take the gamble. Enterprise Zones should encourage experimentation and risk-taking. They should not become tax-free homes for weak companies. Bold departures in policy, on the other hand, may need a long and carefully monitored test period before they are applied across the whole country.

The AIB also put forward the suggestion that the package of incentives should vary among the zones, to compare their success at achieving the objectives of the Enterprise Zones. This is a very important idea, and touches on what may be a fatal flaw in the British model. Although the planning regime may vary within limits from place to place, the basic package of fiscal incentives is fixed. The government has, in effect, crossed its fingers in the hope that it has chosen the right set of concessions to obtain the desired results. The desired result does not seem to be the creation of new enterprises; but even if it truly is, there is considerable doubt that the package actually provides the right incentives to achieve it. There is no flexibility in the tax changes, no means of comparing alternative methods of stimulating the entrepreneurs that are needed. If the measures in the zones do not turn out to be the right ones, and they fail, then the whole approach may be rejected on the basis of one inadequate experiment.

It would have made more sense, as the AIB proposed, to vary the basic incentives in each zone, and to experiment with other changes in cities willing to take the risk. In one zone, a package might have been devised that appealed almost exclusively to small entrepreneurs, with tax incentives for investors in small companies, and concessions for those rehabilitating old buildings. Elsewhere, the tax benefits might have been extended to residential property. In another zone, it might have been a requirement that the city should allow private contractors to provide the usual municipal services. With a range of zones there would no doubt be some failures, as well as some successes. But we would be setting in motion not only an experiment to test the power of free enterprise in dealing with the problems of the inner city, but also the means of finding out what we need to do to unleash it. The British Enterprise Zone model rests on the assumption that the government already knows how to do that, but there is every reason to suppose that it does not.

The British Experiment in Perspective

It is far too early to evaluate the British Enterprise Zone experiment in the sense of any assessment of the economic and social impact of the program. The legislation allowing the government to go ahead with detailed plans for each chosen zone was passed only in November 1980, and it was regarded as unlikely that any of the sites would be fully functional until well into the summer of 1981. Even then, it will take many more months, or years, before any clear picture begins to emerge.

It would not be premature, however, to make some general observations regarding the manner in which the idea of the Enterprise Zone has been transformed into reality in Britain. The

123

objectives and the process of selection of sites is very relevant to the debate in the United States, as is the package of incentives being tested. Even at this early stage, there are many lessons to be learned. But it should be remembered constantly that the zones in Britain are but one version of a general approach which aims to stimulate new economic activity and social improvement in the inner cities through the reduction of government-created obstacles, instead of through government intervention. The British zones are the first models, not the definitive ones, and they should be judged with that in mind.

The objectives of the British Enterprise Zones were made clear during the progress of the legislation. Their purpose is to encourage rapid and significant redevelopment of derelict areas in depressed parts of cities—areas where little economic activity has occurred in recent years despite expensive government programs. The engine of redevelopment in the zones is seen as the private sector, spurred on with the incentives of low tax and the freedom to develop with minimal red tape. If this redevelopment takes place, it is assumed, it will provide a major stimulus to a large urban area, bringing new jobs and prosperity to the region, not merely the zone.

The siting strategy reflects some important differences between inner cities in Britain and in America. There are practically no residents in any of the zones chosen so far, nor are there any incentives aimed at a residential population. The mixed-land-use ideas of Jane Jacobs are not a part of the British model. One reason for this is that the British zones are not even designed to tackle the severe social problems that are a depressingly familiar part of American inner-city neighborhoods. The crime problem associated with distressed areas in American cities is much less severe in Britain, and the zones are not seen as a way of encouraging pioneering small entrepreneurs to begin the slow process of rebuilding the social fabric of a community. The absence of social objectives partly explains the lack of emphasis on small firms. It also explains in part the avoidance of sites with any substantial population. The zones are not seen as a means of integrating residential and business activity, for the benefit of the neighborhood. They are seen only as business zones.

By choosing a small number of sites, the government was able to ensure a measure of competition among the applicants, and also that those picked would be enthusiastic about the concept.

Enthusiasm was considered essential by the government, because cities have to give up much of their planning power within the zones. Unfortunately, there is no mechanism in the zones to channel that enthusiasm into innovative experiments at the local level; no suggestion of trying shop-steading, private services, private streets, or other innovative ideas that would seem to be a part of the general approach.

The British system of government is not federal in nature—ultimate sovereignty rests in Parliament—and so thorny questions of jurisdiction are less of an issue with respect to creating zones than they would be in the United States. Nevertheless, the partnership between the central government and the local authority involved in the zone may give some guidance for the process of reaching agreement in the United States. During the process of site selection, the national government consults with the local council, but it is the council that puts forward the proposal. If the proposal is agreeable to the government, and negotiations succeed in establishing the terms of the zone, then it is the local authority that administers the Enterprise Zone. The site proposal and the administration of the zone are thus the responsibility of the local authority. The national government's role is to ensure that the site meets certain, flexible, standards before the fiscal incentives apply.

The British avoided laying down any precise requirements for areas that might be chosen as zones. No exact criteria were given for size, level of distress, or the rate of unemployment in the district. Only broad guidelines were provided. The government defends this as a way of giving itself more flexibility in choosing a range of locations that would provide a good basis for an experiment. Officials also argue that the lack of hard-and-fast criteria gives greater freedom to draw boundaries in the most sensible manner for the area, rather than have to keep to census tracts or some similarly artificial dividing line.

But there are two sides to discretion. There is the very worthy argument of flexibility. There is also the danger that the choice of site can become a political favor. The record of UDAG and the Model Cities program in America demonstrates the reality of discretion, and it is worth noting that the distribution of the British zones reflects a strong political as well as economic rationale. Nevertheless, it is difficult to see how a designation process could be made truly automatic, and free from political considerations, without also making it so blind that it would ignore local conditions.

The local commitment of the Enterprise Zone in Britain is confined to the zoning or planning permission process. By agreeing to reimburse abated property taxes, the central government removed in advance the resistance that would no doubt emerge had councils been required to reduce taxes within the zones. By also agreeing to reimburse lost tax on *new* developments, the cental government went a stage further than merely covering the local councils for losses on existing structures. It not only diffused the criticism that councils would suffer a net loss of tax if relocation took place within the city, but gave an additional incentive to cities to attract companies into the zones. The more business that is attracted, the larger is the check from the Treasury. The government is fully aware that this is an open-minded commitment, but it is seen as a necessary financial inducement to cities to play a leading role in trying to make the zones work.

Despite these interesting aspects of the British zones, it is still apparent that the British Enterprise Zones are a much less bold departure than it seemed they would be when the concept was first unveiled. They have little to do with new, innovative entrepreneurs and much to do with established corporations and real estate developers. Rather than encourage capital to flow into new businesses, they seem destined to be areas where big companies are given tax breaks to grow bigger still. Britain has very substantial tax allowances designed to encourage companies to reinvest their profits, and this has led to capital being locked into old, slowly growing businesses, rather than being made available in the capital market for new, fast-growing firms. The creation of Enterprise Zones, with their tax write-offs for mature companies, may turn out to be just a stronger dose of the same medicine that has left Britain with the old, stagnant economy and very low job generation.

Most experiments do fail, but it would be a tragedy if the Enterprise Zones fail in Britain because the tax mechanism on which they are founded is faulty, while the basic idea of unleashing the private sector in the inner cities is actually very sound. If the criticisms voiced by the small-business sector in Britain prove well-founded, there could be increased commercial and industrial activity within the zones, but it will tend to be at the expense of other places. With the structure of incentives now in place, we might expect to see Enterprise Zones where well-financed growing companies, enjoying substantial tax benefits, compete with small local businesses outside the zones. That would hardly fit the image of Hong Kongs in the inner cities, and it would not be very beneficial to either the local or the national economy. Without a strong emphasis on small new businesses, there can be little genuine enterprise in Enterprise Zones.

In order to monitor the progress of its zones, the British government has appointed a team of consultants to study the effects they have on the local economy. As the results come in from the experiment, the conditions in the zones may likely be modified. It already seems that some size restrictions will be applied to retailing outlets in the zones, in view of the problems already encountered. Although such adjustments may be necessary, there is always the danger that we may end up with a body of new regulations and restrictions to replace the old ones, simply as a consequence of incentives that lead to undesired results.

The British Enterprise Zones are not places in the inner city where the door has been thrown open to unfettered free enterprise. In truth, the door has only been opened partly to one segment of free enterprise, and it is far from clear that it is the right segment to achieve an economic rebirth of the inner cities. The door still appears to be firmly closed against the small entrepreneurs who offer the best hope for the innovative ideas and jobs that are needed.

NOTES

1. Speech to the Royal Town Planning Institute, 15 June 1977. The following quotations by Peter Hall are taken from the speech.
2. Speech to the Bow Group, 26 June 1978. The following quotations by Sir Geoffrey Howe are taken from the speech.
3. The Tribune Group is a caucus of left-wing Labour Party members of Parliament. They tend to be the strongest critics of everything the Conservatives stand for.
4. The Employment Protection Act had been heavily criticized by business groups on the grounds that the tight restrictions placed on the freedom of employers to dismiss employees made them extremely reluctant to hire workers, thus increasing unemployment rather than reducing it.
5. *Financial Times*, 29 June 1978.
6. Madsen Pirie, "A Short History of Enterprise Zones," *National Review*, 23 January 1981, p. 28.
7. Her Majesty's Treasury statement, London, 26 March 1980.

8. Joint Report of the Chief Executive and City Planning Officer, City of Liverpool, 27 August 1980.
9. *Daily Telegraph*, 29 March 1980.
10. *The Economist*, 29 March 1980.
11. Speech in the House of Commons, 4 June 1980.
12. Quoted in the *Financial Times*, 30 July 1980.
13. Quoted in *Enterprise Zones* (National Executive Committee on the Labour Party, London, 1980), p. 6.
14. *Ibid.*, p. 1.
15. *Financial Times*, 27 November 1980.
16. *Birmingham Post*, 27 November 1980.
17. *County Express*, 5 December 1980.
18. *The Observer*, 3 August 1978.
19. *Loughborough Monitor*, 17 December 1980.
20. *Dudley Herald*, 5 December 1980.
21. *County Express*, 28 November 1980.
22. *NOW!*, 24 November 1980.
23. *Parliamentary Debates (House of Commons)*, Standing Committee D, 20 May 1980, cols. 1258, 1259, 1264.
24. *The Economist*, 3 January 1981, p. 54.
25. *Ibid.*
26. *CBI Response to the Government's Consultative Document on Enterprise Zones* (CBI, London, June 1980).
27. *Comment on Enterprise Zone Policy Proposals* (AIB, London, May 1980).

5. CREATING ENTERPRISE ZONES IN AMERICA

A Coalition Forms

It is not surprising that an idea which sought to apply a private enterprise approach to the problem of inner city blight attracted strong interest in the United States. The concept was first introduced to America early in 1979 by the Washington-based Heritage Foundation in the form of a short analysis of the zone ideas put forward by Peter Hall and Sir Geoffrey Howe.[1] The concept immediately aroused the interest of legislators and the media.

The thought of trying a radical free market approach in blighted neighborhoods where government programs are not working caught the imagination of many people. Advocates of free enterprise saw an opportunity to unleash the latent capitalistic instincts that they believe exist in even the most depressed neighborhoods. The idea of creating a Taiwan in the Bronx held out the opportunity of showing just what the market economy is capable of achieving in even the most unfavorable circumstances. Although most liberals doubted that the results would be as spectacular as conservatives predicted, they had to agree that since existing efforts do not seem to be working, little could be lost in trying something radically different.

The Enterprise Zone concept had another advantage as a policy—its apparent low cost. Removing regulation and tax burdens on business in places where there is no business does not constitute a loss. Conservatives found the absence of "up front" money very attractive. And although tax breaks might arguably constitute a tax loss to the government (very arguably, it might be added, since *new* business would add revenue, even if the rates were lower), the loss would result only from businesses actually starting up in the zones. The pay-out of so-called tax expenditures, in other words, would occur only with success. Unlike government grants, renewal projects and the like, the Treasury was not being asked to spend money in the *hope* of success.

Liberals had a similar reason for supporting the Enterprise Zone. If the concept did not involve considerable expenditures, then even if they were skeptical of its success it would be worth trying, since it would not pull resources away from other programs. Enterprise Zones could be added to programs aimed at highly blighted areas. If they really were successful, money could be transferred from projects that were totally ineffective and concentrated into others that could boast results.

Within two months of the Enterprise Zone idea reaching the United States, a bill embodying the concept had been introduced in the Illinois General Assembly by Representative Don Totten. The bill authorized the Illinois Department of Business and Economic Development to create Enterprise Zones in depressed areas of the state. Within the zones the Department would establish minimum guidelines regarding zoning, health, and safety codes. All land owned by the state or a local government in the designated zones would have to be sold at auction, and all state and local laws dealing with building codes, zoning, prices, and wages would be superseded by the Department's guidelines. In addition, property taxes would not be collected in the first year of operation of any zone, but the taxes would be phased back in over a period of five years.

Despite the radical nature of the Illinois bill, it received strong support. Under pressure from organized labor, the provision suspending the state minimum wage was dropped, and the amended bill passed the House very comfortably. It failed in the Senate, however, on a tie vote.

The enthusiasm shown for the Illinois bill was much greater than even its sponsors had ever thought likely, and it encouraged the American Legislative Exchange Council, a national organization of state legislators, to include a *pro forma* Enterprise Zone bill in its annual handbook of suggested state legislation.[2] In 1980, most state legislatures convened for only a short session prior to the election, and so there was little movement on the idea at the state level during the year. In the 1981 session, however, legislators in a number of states introduced bills providing for significant reduction in state regulation and taxes within selected distressed areas.

Interest in the U.S. Congress took only a little longer to emerge, but the idea received a critical boost when it was taken up by Jack Kemp, the tax-cutting, conservative Republican from Buffalo, N.Y. In May 1980, Kemp introduced a version of the Enterprise Zone in a bill laid before the House.[3] Although liberal congressmen may rarely vote with Kemp, he nevertheless has a reputation as an innovative and intelligent legislator, and so there was considerable interest in his bill from both sides of the aisle. But it was still something of a surprise when Kemp managed to persuade Robert Garcia, the liberal Democrat representing the blighted South Bronx, to join him in a revised version of the bill, introduced in June.

The Kemp-Garcia bill was a major step forward for the Enterprise Zone idea in America. The partnership itself made it respectable for politicians and interest groups of widely differing viewpoints to support the concept. The symbolism of the Kemp-Garcia partnership was also not lost on the media. But the coalition was a lot more than a symbolic political gesture. It was a clear demonstration that the underlying theme of the Enterprise Zone spanned the political spectrum. It implied genuine agreement that the only way of achieving a sound and sustained renewal of depressed inner city neighborhoods is to make them once again attractive to enterprising businesses, so that real private jobs will be created.

The Kemp-Garcia Urban Jobs and Enterprise Zone Act[4] sought to make inner-city areas more attractive to business development by reducing the tax burdens on companies locating in designated parts of depressed neighborhoods. The purpose was to create a climate conducive to enterprise. Where the business world had *redlined* an area—written it off, in other words—the Enterprise Zone, according to Kemp, would have the effect of *greenlining* it—making it a place where people would be encouraged to take risks and create jobs.

For an area to be designated an Enterprise Zone under the bill, a local government would have to recommend a location that met certain eligibility criteria laid down in the measure. Unemployment and poverty would have to be substantially higher than the national average, and the potential zone would have to contain at least 4,000 people. The local government administering the area would also have to agree to a reduction in real property taxes of at least 20% within four years. If that undertaking was given, the Secretary of Commerce was authorized under the bill to designate the area an Enterprise Jobs Zone for a period of at least ten years.

Once the designation was awarded, certain federal incentives would apply in the zone. Whether or not he was a resident, anyone investing in the area would be able to take an increased capital gain deduction on any appreciation of assets in the zone. Employees performing most of their duties in an Enterprise Zone would be subject to lower social security taxes. If the employee was below 21 years of age, the employer and employee contribution would be cut by 90%; if the employee was over 21, a 50% reduction applied. The shortfall in the fund was to be made up out of general revenues.

If half of the employees of a zone company performed most of their duties in the zone, and at least half of these employees actually lived in the zone, then the Kemp-Garcia bill gave substantial additional tax breaks to the company. Such firms would receive a 15% reduction in corporate income tax. Up to half a million dollars a year in capital equipment invested in the zone could be written off against taxable income over just three years, and losses sustained by the business could be carried forward for up to ten years.

The Kemp-Garcia bill also included a Sense of the Congress provision designed to simplify the procedure for setting up a foreign trade zone within an Enterprise Zone. Normally, the Foreign Trade Zone Board of the Department of Commerce requires the local government wanting a zone to demonstrate that facilities and business conditions are sufficiently developed in an area for it to take full advantage of a customs-free trade zone. The bill, however, requires the Board to consider not the present conditions when deciding on an application, but conditions that would exist by virtue of the foreign trade zone. In other words, the foreign trade zone in an Enterprise Zone was seen by the bill as a mechanism for lifting a neighborhood out of blight and depression, and not as an addition to an already mature local economy.

The sponsors of the Kemp-Garcia bill made it clear that they did not see it as a finished piece of legislative work. It was intended primarily as a discussion document—as a focus for debate on the concept of the Enterprise Zone. There was no attempt by the bill's originators to push it forward for a decision by the Congress, or to subject it to close scrutiny in hearings. Suggestions and criticisms were welcomed, and it was assumed that a revised version, based on such observations, would be introduced in the 1981 Congress.

Two broad sets of criticisms began to emerge. One set could be classed as conceptual questions, which will be discussed later. These involved issues such as relocation, displacement, "unfair" competition from zone firms, and the like. Such criticisms were not particularly applicable to the Kemp-Garcia bill any more than to any other version of the idea, but since the bill had become the centerpiece for discussion on the topic, these criticisms were directed to it.

Other criticisms were of a more technical nature, although even these, in part, challenged some of the basic elements of the Enterprise Zone idea. Some, in effect, disputed the whole assumption of the bill, that new enterprises would be encouraged by business tax breaks. According to William Dennis of NFIB, America's most powerful small business lobby, "Kemp thinks if we just marginally lower the costs of doing business in these areas, millions of small businesses will suddenly bloom. It just isn't going to happen."[5]

The reason it won't happen, argued small businessmen, is that depreciation allowances, cuts in corporate income tax, and similar business tax breaks are a significant incentive only to existing businesses that are making money and paying taxes. Most new firms are not in this happy position—they may operate for years before they can take any real advantage of the benefits offered in the bill. The property tax reduction and social security tax cut would be of some help, small businessmen admitted, but the major breaks would be of only marginal use. What the small entrepreneur needs is capital and a reduction in red tape. Yet the Kemp-Garcia bill addressed neither of these.

The criticisms of small businessmen in the United States were very reminiscent of those voiced by their British counterparts. Cutting business taxes is not the same as creating a climate for new enterprise. Measures aimed at encouraging the reinvestment of earnings by existing companies might cause them to grow, and some would relocate into the zone to receive such encouragement; but this is not the kind of incentive that a small, new firm needs.

Arguments of this nature were given some support by a number of detailed analyses of the bill. George Sternlieb of Rutgers University, for example, argued in a study for the Commerce Department that the companies with most to gain from the Kemp-Garcia incentives would be those with heavy tax bills that were also considering large capital investments.[6] The zones, Sternlieb argued, would tend to become tax havens for such firms, rather than centers for new, job-generating small firms.

Even some of the measures in the bill that seemed certain to help smaller firms came under attack. Sternlieb's study, for instance, concluded that the social security tax cut would have only a small effect on the labor costs of most small firms. The greatest beneficiaries, he claimed, would be employees with high incomes. So the measure might actually create more openings for highly paid executives than for unskilled workers! Steering a selective reduction in social security tax through the Congress was in any case seen as a battle in itself, given the precarious state of the fund and the unwillingness of most congressmen to subsidize it from general revenues. Even Senator John Chafee, one of the bill's sponsors in the Senate, and a leading member of the Finance Committee, expressed strong doubts that the Senate would go along with such an idea.

The requirement that a proportion of a company's employees must reside in a zone before the firm could gain the most significant benefits was also attacked as impractical. It was seen by some as just the kind of regulation that Enterprise Zones were supposed to remove. Nobody goes into business in order to hire people, and critics felt that telling an entrepreneur whom he must hire would be the last straw for the kind of individualistic businessmen being sought. In addition, the prospect of government agents raiding firms to check the residence of employees was thought unlikely to be attractive to companies, to say the least. And what if a company was close to the lower limit of local employees? If a worker from the ghetto had moved up the economic ladder and wanted to live somewhere more pleasant, should he be fired so that the firm could keep its quota of locals?

The inclusion of a residency requirement was certainly well-meaning. If the aim of the Enterprise Zone is to create employment and opportunity in the inner city, then it might seem reasonable to try to guarantee it in the language of a law. But trying to ensure success through restrictions is actually more likely to destroy the chances of achieving it, because it means putting more reins on the entrepreneur. If the Enterprise Zone does not create jobs for local people, then there is either something very wrong with the basic idea or with the incentive mechanism chosen as a foundation for the zone. If that is the case, it should be scrapped or the incentives should be modified. But if both are sound, imposing hiring restrictions will only blunt and distort the development process. Trying to regulate entrepreneurs into delivering the results one wants is always less effective than providing them with the right incentives.

The property tax requirement in the Kemp-Garcia bill also came under fire. In several states it is unconstitutional for a city to have differing rates of property tax within its boundaries, and so these states would be ruled out automatically as locations for Enterprise Zones. Many financially strapped cities further complained that reducing taxes was unthinkable—every dollar of revenue is necessary.

Although the constitutional objection to this provision of the bill held great force, the revenue argument had much less merit. The Enterprise Zone is designed to deal with the problems of very distressed areas, where there is little activity and considerable abandonment. These areas yield very little tax revenue, despite the rates that apply (and to a great extent *because* of the rates that apply). In many cases, abandonment is accelerated by assessments that cannot be paid. This adds to the erosion of the tax base and increases the pressure for higher rates. But reducing the tax rate on property in the area may actually increase the revenue, because of increased business activity and property values. There always seems to be a confusion at City Hall that cutting a tax *rate* necessarily means cutting the tax *yield*. Few businessmen would fall for that argument. If a company overprices its goods and none are selling, a cut in prices will generate a least *some* revenue. Similarly, if a city "overprices" its property taxes, a cut will be the most effective way to increase revenue while simultaneously increasing activity.

The lack of any move to streamline regulation in the Kemp-Garcia bill was seen by some as a serious flaw, given the stated intention of stimulating new enterprise. It is not that the basic pollution or safety standards are a major obstacle, but rather that the complexity and staggering volume of the whole array of government regulation is an onerous and unnecessary additional burden to place on a small businessman contemplating an operation in a bad neighborhood.

But the very thought of streamlining regulation, or of cutting minimum wage and other supposed protections, sends shock waves through the Enterprise Zone coalition. Many of the Democrats supporting the concept have fought for years to achieve what they believe to be vital safeguards. These same legislators could hardly be expected to endorse a measure that removed these safeguards in parts of their own districts. Most conservative and business supporters of the Enterprise Zone appreciate the political sensitivity of reducing regulation in a zone. Even Jack Kemp did not advocate the inclusion in the bill of any significant changes in regulation. As NFIB lobbyist John Motley has explained, "What we have here is a very delicate political alliance. The things that would really attract small businessmen to Enterprise Zones are exemptions from regulations and the minimum wage. But they would probably throw the alliance into disarray."[7]

There does, indeed, seem to be an unpleasant dilemma facing the Enterprise Zone. The relaxation of regulation appears to be an essential ingredient of any package aimed at encouraging small business creation in depressed neighborhoods. And yet, the support of the political forces representing those neighborhoods is crucial for the Enterprise Zone approach to succeed.

There may be more scope for sensible regulatory change in Enterprise Zones, however, than is generally perceived. There is broad agreement that a certain regulatory instrument may be proper for an industry as a whole, but that the same instrument may be unreasonable in the case of small companies or jurisdictions. The unequal effect of regulations was recognized in the Regulatory Flexibility Act, enacted in September 1980.[8] Passed with the strong support of many leading liberals, the preamble admits that, "Uniform Federal regulatory and reporting requirements have in numerous instances imposed unnecessary and disproportionately burdensome demands, including legal, accounting and consulting costs upon small organizations, and small governmental jurisdictions with limited resources."[9]

The Act established what is, in practice, a two-tiered approach to regulation, under which agencies are required to examine the impact of a proposed regulation on "small entities." If the regulation seems likely to have a significant adverse effect on a "substantial number" of such small entities, the agency must consider alternative means of achieving the goals of the applicable statute. This may mean excluding small entities from the rule altogether, or the application of a different mechanism. Existing regulations must be examined on the same basis within the next ten years.

The Act has the effect of relieving small companies of some of the burden of regulations that are not designed for them, but which impose hardship. It does not exempt such companies from the thrust of the legislation leading to the regulations, but allows agencies to design alternative and simpler mechanisms that take into account the problems small entities have in complying with many regulations.

The Regulatory Flexibility Act may prove to be sufficient as a vehicle for reducing the regulatory burden on new enterprises in an Enterprise Zone, through its impact on small companies in general. But perhaps the Act could be taken further, by amendment or interpretation, without losing liberal support. If an Enterprise Zone were considered a "small entity" under the terms of the Act, it would open up the possibility of a flexible approach to regulation within the zones.[10] This would not mean that the *intent* of statutes safeguarding people within zones would be eroded, but only that agencies would be required to seek alternative, simpler means to achieve these goals. So we might see Enterprise Zones with a modified body of regulation operating within them, designed to stimulate entrepreneurial activity while protecting the public.

Although the streamlining of federal regulations may be important for the encouragement of new business in an Enterprise Zone, it is generally agreed that perhaps the greatest bureaucratic obstacles exist at the local level. Zoning, building codes, permits and other restrictions serve to push up the cost of new activity, or to prevent it. Yet the Kemp-Garcia bill contained no provision that required cities to modify, or eliminate, such restrictions. The sponsors pointed out that it would be extremely difficult to devise legal language that could have applied to all places where an Enterprise Zone might be sited—even if it was accepted that such a provision would be helpful. It would be better, they argued, to accept that the federal government can go only so far in the process of creating Enterprise Zones, and allow state and city governments to deal with the local aspects of the idea.

Congressmen Kemp and Garcia have been remodeling their bill in the light of the discussions that the original version provoked. At the time of writing the new Kemp-Garcia bill had not been presented to Congress, but it was expected during the summer of 1981. It seemed likely that it would contain some very important modifications resulting from the criticisms and suggestions that were received. The requirement that cities must reduce property taxes within the zones would almost certainly disappear. In its place there was likely to be some form of contract requirement, whereby the city would have to assemble a package of local incentives, acceptable to the federal government, to match the federal changes. The idea of such a contract will be discussed later in this chapter.

The new Kemp-Garcia bill was expected to include some other key refinements. It appeared that a form of employment tax credit, geared toward disadvantaged workers or the structurally unemployed, would replace the social security tax cut in the original bill. In addition, an application of the Regulatory Flexibility Act to Enterprise Zones was considered closely by the sponsors, and it was likely to become a feature of the new bill.

Although Congressmen Kemp and Garcia have succeeded in making their proposals the center of debate on the Enterprise Zone, the adoption of the concept by Ronald Reagan during the presidential campaign may eventually shift the focus of interest to the White House. In his well-publicized campaign stop in the South Bronx, in his speech to the Urban League, and during the presidential debates, candidate Reagan made the promise that the Enterprise Zone concept would be a crucial part of his urban policy. A White House task force was created soon after his inauguration, so that the idea could be studied in detail. It is possible that a pilot project, launched by the Administration in cooperation with selected cities, may lead to the establishment of a number of Enterprise Zones before any legislation passes the Congress. Several cities have already shown interest in the idea. Mayor Koch of New York has endorsed the Enterprise Zone, and so has Mayor Schaefer of Baltimore. And many more cities have indicated that they would like to be among the chosen sites for any experimental scheme.

The Enterprise Zone idea has acquired its own momentum; it is no longer just an interesting urban concept. Conferences are being held around the country, sponsored by widely differing organizations. Cities have task forces working on the proposal, and various bills have appeared at the state and congressional level. But while there may be broad agreement on the broad thrust of the approach, there is not yet a consensus on just how to implement it.

Enterprise Zones in America— A Possible Model

OBJECTIVES

- Job Creation in Depressed Neighborhoods

The creation of employment for inner city residents is seen by all proponents of the Enterprise Zone as the principal goal of the concept. The evidence shows that the small business sector is the most effective generator of the kind of jobs needed, and that the best method of encouraging small enterprise development is not through direct government assistance, but by creating a *climate* in which obstacles to business creation are removed and tax incentives are provided that improve the flow of capital into such new firms.

Although new, small companies are seen as the principal source of job-creation in the inner cities, it is well understood that larger corporations can play an important role, even though they may provide few direct jobs. A major company can play a crucial part as an anchor in a community, as a base on which smaller companies can thrive. Larger companies providing technical services for the small sector may also be invaluable to the growth of new firms. But experience shows that such companies are not sensitive to the "climate" approach of the Enterprise Zone. Location decisions by larger companies are complex, and a city needs to assemble a package of incentives if it is to succeed in bringing such a firm into a depressed neighborhood. This has to be done on a case-by-case basis, and it is best done at the local level. The Enterprise Zone is not an appropriate mechanism to do this. If the federal tax incentives are strengthened to the degree that they become the overriding factor in location decisions by major corporations, they are going to provide a field day for corporate accountants seeking to use the zones as tax havens for their clients. If a city feels that a major corporation should be a feature of an Enterprise Zone, it should deal with the firm on an individual basis.

- Expanding the Economy

Although the creation of jobs and business opportunities in the inner city is the underlying theme of the Enterprise Zone, it should not seek to achieve this at the expense of other parts of the nation. It is *not* the purpose of the Enterprise Zone to bring about a redistribution of economic activity for the benefit of people who happen to live in particular neighborhoods. It would be difficult to justify the idea if that was the intended result, since that would weaken the national economy.

What the Enterprise Zone *does* try to do is to allow the latent strengths of a neighborhood to be fully used for its own improvement—to enable it to make the best use of what it has. It tries to create an environment of opportunity, in which old buildings, idle capital, unemployed people, and local entrepreneurship can become productive. The purpose, in short, is to *add* to the national economy by removing obstacles that stifle creative activity, not to reallocate the fruits of the economy.

- Encouraging Local Enterprise

Creating jobs is not the only proper goal of the Enterprise Zone. Creating opportunities for local enterprise is also an essential feature of the idea. It is necessary to break the underclass mentality that characterizes the residents of most depressed neighborhoods—particularly in minority neighborhoods—causing people to believe that economic opportunity has passed them by. This pessimism itself is a major cause of decline, and no neighborhood can be turned around until the people within it begin to feel that it is possible, and worthwhile, to build up businesses. Relying on outsiders to provide the jobs may create jobs quickly, but it will not necessarily lead to the development of the local business class needed for stable development—it may even lead to tension and the sort of racial explosion we have seen in Liberty City and elsewhere. Since the residents of depressed neighborhoods, almost by

140

definition, lack the skills and resources to start large, sophisticated businesses, the zone must make it simple and inexpensive for small businesses to be established.

Although the development of a business class in a poor neighborhood is a lengthy process, it would be wrong to believe that there is an absence of talent. In most depressed inner-city districts there is a thriving underground economy. This does not mean only criminal activity. If you are prepared to pay cash, it is usually very easy to have your car fixed, or your house painted—enterprise does occur if the returns are sufficient! The idea of the Enterprise Zone is to encourage such entrepreneurs to become legitimate, to set up workshops, and to employ others. That is the only way to build a solid foundation, and to enable business skills to be passed on to others.

- Social Improvement

Economic rejuvenation is the principal theme of the zones, but this is unlikely to occur without parallel improvements in the social climate within depressed neighborhoods. The climate of enterprise must therefore be seen as extending beyond the economic field. Neighborhoods have shown themselves well able to develop innovative self-help projects if they are allowed to exercise control over them.

By giving neighborhood organizations greater freedom to provide services such as security, day care centers and the like, it is possible to strengthen the social fabric of an area. This makes the neighborhood more attractive to entrepreneurs, and the existence of these businessmen adds to the process of improvement. This informal coalition of small entrepreneurs with a financial stake in the district, and the range of official and unofficial organizations that exist, are the agents of improvement that the Enterprise Zone should seek to encourage.

- Innovation and Experimentation

The Enterprise Zone may almost be described as a process of "unplanning" city neighborhoods, in that no preconceived physical, social, or economic plan is imposed. But it would be more accurate to see the zones as a conscious attempt to set in motion a dynamic *process*—the process of continuous experimentation and adaption. This is unplanned in the sense that there is no central direction. But each person in the process plans according to his perception of the situation and the goals he has. The net effect of this process of individual planning and risk-taking is that ideas are tested and compared, leading to improved businesses and services for the neighborhood.

The encouragement of experimentation is important at many levels. It enables new methods of delivering services to the neighborhood to be discovered. Many declining cities are locked into ways of providing services that cannot be financed adequately with the existing tax base. Instead of new methods being tested, poorer services are provided. Those cities that have tried innovative alternatives have often combined significant savings with improved efficiency and satisfaction. The Enterprise Zone should be a center for such innovation, for the benefit of the whole city.

The value of small-scale experimentation in public policy is not confined to the provision of city services. Many policy ideas have been put forward as possible ways of alleviating the problems of the inner city, such as housing vouchers, a reverse income tax, and the suspension of the minimum wage. Many of these ideas are controversial, and there is honest disagreement over what their effects would be. The Enterprise Zone would provide an ideal laboratory to test some of these ideas in the field. It would not be a typical urban situation, of course, if Enterprise Zones really were confined to the most depressed areas, and this would have to be taken into account in assessing the results. But such experiments could hardly be accused of replacing something that works with unknown policies. We would be testing radical, innovative approaches in locations where the residents had a great deal to gain if the experiment were a success, and very little to lose if it failed.

The idea of systematically testing new policies in certain urban areas has recently been suggested by a number of mayors. Mayor Koch of New York and Mayor Bradley of Los Angeles, for instance, put forward their cities as possible sites for a limited test of a subminimum youth wage before any national measure is contemplated. Mayor Schaefer of Baltimore, in a memorandum to Mr. Reagan just before the inauguration, even went so far as to suggest that the government should consider establishing Baltimore as a "laboratory city," for the testing of new urban initiatives.[11]

Systematic experimentation in an Enterprise Zone would seem to be a logical extension of this, and would allow more radical ideas to be examined within a limited area.

Creating the climate for innovation and experimentation within an Enterprise Zone would also be beneficial for the national economy. Cities were once the centers of business innovation. And for good reason. Close at hand there were inexpensive "make-do" old buildings in which new ideas could be incubated. There was a pool of capital and talent that the entrepreneur could use, and a large market he could sell to. But the costs and restrictions we have imposed on urban enterprise has tended to drive out more creative people and caused them to move to small towns and to other regions of the country that are more welcoming. The Enterprise Zone, however, would be a haven for such people, where new, high-risk ideas could be tried with the minimum of fuss and unnecessary cost.

THE FRAMEWORK

The Enterprise Zones would spur development by creating a climate of opportunity in depressed neighborhoods through the reduction of regulation, taxes, and other government-imposed costs. These obstacles are not the exclusive result of the federal government, however, and it is necessary to effect change at various levels of government. This is no simple task. In the United States it requires a mechanism that can operate in fifty states, each with its own laws, and in cities that also have a wide diversity of local laws and regulations. A federal Enterprise Zone law which would seek to fill all these conditions would be very complex, and almost certainly ineffective.

A more productive approach to the problem might be the idea of a negotiated *contract* between the federal government and the city. The revised Kemp-Garcia bill provides for such a contract, and it is the basis of the British model—although in Britain it is limited to the process of establishing the boundaries and the zoning conditions. A general package of federal tax and regulatory changes would be available for any location suggested by a city that met certain federal criteria regarding distress, *providing* the city agreed to match the federal concessions with a combination of changes at the local level—probably in cooperation with the state. The federal government, from its side of the bargaining table,

143

would in the first instance be offering the standard package of concessions, and pressing the city to offer local changes in return. The city, from its side, would see itself as "paying" for the federal incentives.

It might be that no bargain could be struck. The city might feel that the price was too high, in which case there would be either no Enterprise Zone at all, or a purely local version with no federal element. In Britain, some of the short-listed cities withdrew their applications when they concluded that the concessions required were too extensive for them to accept. But if a contract could be made, where the basic federal changes were matched by local changes acceptable to both sides, then an Enterprise Zone would come into being. The contract would run for a period of time agreeable to both sides, or be laid down in the enabling legislation. As in the British model, it would make good sense to allow for the contract to be terminated or amended with the agreement of both sides. It would then be possible to improve the zone in the light of experience, or to end it if it was not having desirable effects.

Once the basic Enterprise Zone contract had been agreed upon, however, it would be possible for the bargaining process to continue. Additional changes and incentives could be agreed on between the parties with the aim of creating an even more attractive entrepreneurial climate in the zone. It is most unlikely that the U.S. Congress would ever allow the tax code to become a subject of negotiation with cities, but it might be possible for the federal government to offer other concessions or experimental urban programs, in return for further local incentives for the zone. Some elements of a "superzone" might be linked together. The federal government, for instance, might agree to introduce a system of housing vouchers or rent assistance into the zone on condition that the city eliminated rent control within the zone's borders. Other elements of the contract might be quite unconnected. An agreement by the city to allow private companies to provide garbage collection services, for example, might be matched by an agreement to establish a foreign trade zone or to introduce an experimental negative income tax for zone residents.

Under this approach to the creation and design of Enterprise Zones, a whole range of different zones would be possible. In very cautious cities, there might be only a "standard" zone, with a basic package of federal and local changes. Even in such zones, the local commitment might vary. Elsewhere, there would be more radical zones, where cities were willing to offer more significant concessions in return for more innovative federal proposals.

This variety in the zones would be very valuable. It would enable different mechanisms to be tested and compared, and it would allow the style of the zone to fit the local circumstances of the city. It might be that elements of some versions would prove to be very successful, and these might become a standard feature of future zones. Other experimental ideas might be dismal failures, and be withdrawn by agreement. Some of the ideas tested in the zones might also be judged to be appropriate as a part of national urban policy and be legislated into a general program. A range of Enterprise Zones, in other words, would constitute experimentation in itself, with the continuous process of experimentation and comparison serving to improve the general mechanism.

The idea of zones emerging out of negotiation rather than out of cooperation between levels of government is important, since it would tend to lead to a more efficient method of design. It is not so much that different levels of the federal system are in conflict, but rather that they represent often opposing constituencies. The federal government can offer targeted incentives, but wants the cities and the states to make changes that might be politically unpalatable. The city, on the other hand, wants the federal incentives but will avoid local changes as far as it can. A "bargaining" approach to this political reality is far more likely to lead to a successful program than any attempt at a "joint" endeavor.

The "Standard" Federal Package

In developing legislation to create Enterprise Zones, the federal government must accomplish two things. First, it must lay down criteria for the selection and administration of the zones. And, second, it must provide a basic package of tax and other incentives that would be a standard foundation for all the zones.

The selection criteria depend very much on whether the zones are seen as a limited, experimental program, or as a program that is deemed applicable to *any* area meeting certain conditions. If the former, then precise targeting requirements are not really necessary, since there would be a conscious attempt to pick a range of sites suitable for a test program. The British program is such an

145

experimental approach, and no precise requirements were laid down. Limiting the number of sites has some advantage, even if it is only the prelude to a general program. It would mean that cities would have to compete for selection, and so there would be a greater pressure on them to accept more radical local changes. This would provide a good demonstration of this approach. If the Enterprise Zone were launched as a general program, however, it would result in "softer" zones, since the federal government could not lay down requirements that only a few cities would be willing to meet.

A general program does require more precise targeting requirements, if it is not to be subject to favoritism and other abuses. Laying down watertight requirements is a tricky business, as the drafters of the Kemp-Garcia legislation know all too well. The more exact one makes the language, the less it can take account of local factors. Although there is always danger in discretion at the federal level, the only workable approach would seem to be to lay down broad guidelines regarding the degree of distress that must occur in an area for it to be considered, and for the final decision on any application to be made by the federal government. Although this would no doubt lead to favored cities being awarded zones in questionable locations, it would also enable the boundaries of zones to be chosen by people, rather than by computers that have little understanding of communities.

The size of a zone would depend on the neighborhood, but in the first instance, it should be small—say a square mile or so. This is not because the beneficial effects of the zones should be reserved for just a few people. It is because the idea is experimental, and we should be able to compare the effects of the zone with the effects of other programs in the same neighborhood. In addition, the zone concept is designed for highly depressed sections of a city, where tax rates can be cut with little loss to the government. If a zone were to include large numbers of established, profitable companies, the loss could be considerable. If a zone was successful in a limited part of a poor neighborhood, however, it could be expanded at a later date to include more of the neighborhood. If the zone was not effective, keeping it small would at least limit the dashed hopes. Like any new approach, it would be better to start an Enterprise Zone program on a small scale, rather than to include every part of every depressed neighborhood.

It would be sensible to vary the kind of site, at least to some degree. In Britain, the zones are generally located in vacant areas of a city. The general thinking in the United States, however, has been to see them in populated urban areas. But it makes sense to encourage variety and then compare the effects. Some zones should be located on derelict land, some in places where huge old factories could be converted into "condominium" workshops. Others should be in places that have reached rock bottom, while other zones should be in places that had pockets of life. Choosing a range of sites would allow us to find out where the Enterprise Zones would be most effective.

The ideal life-span for an Enterprise Zone depends very much on the incentives given within it. Many would argue that the only reason for any cutoff at all should be to allow a zone to be terminated if it is not being successful. If an Enterprise Zone is benefiting the neighborhood, it would seem to make little sense to end the designation—why stop something that is working for a change?

If the tax incentives in an Enterprise Zone are geared toward the start-up of new companies, and the birthrate of firms improves, then there is a good argument for making the zone permanent. But if many of the incentives are aimed at well-established firms, then the argument for permanent zones is much weaker, since major firms would then be able to use the benefits available in the zone in order to compete with non-zone companies. If an Enterprise Zone were to prosper at the expense of other areas it would be wrong to see it as anything more than a short-term boost to the depressed neighborhood.

A possible way of accommodating these differing possible results would be to set a time limit for the zone, after which it could be extended or phased out over a reasonable period. The initial guaranteed life span would have to be long enough for entrepreneurs to see that it was worth taking the risk of establishing in the zone, and yet short enough to contain any undesirable effects. A consensus seems to have developed on both sides of the Atlantic that ten to fifteen years would be appropriate for these purposes.

As mentioned earlier, the procedure adopted under the 1980 Regulatory Flexibility Act would seem to be a politically effective way of streamlining federal regulation in the Enterprise Zones. If the zones were defined as "small entities" within the terms of the

Act, regulatory agencies would need to consider the special circumstances of the neighborhoods when designing rules. A flexible rule-making approach to Enterprise Zones does not in any way imply that they would be unsafe areas, or places where workers would be exploited. It means simply that an *alternative* set of regulations would be used to achieve the purposes of Congress— regulations that could take into account the features of the zone neighborhood and the goal of creating new activity. A flexible approach would also not let larger concerns off the hook. It could well be that the normal body of regulation would apply to all zone firms above a certain size. It depends entirely on what structure of regulation would be most effective.

The tax incentives in the Enterprise Zones should obviously comply with the aims of the zones and with our present state of knowledge regarding the effectiveness of tax incentives as a means of stimulating new business activity. They should be aimed primarily at small, start-up companies. Even though large companies are important as anchors, it is clear that broad tax incentives are not the best mechanism to draw them into depressed areas.

But it is also clear that new companies are also not very sensitive to business tax incentives. The lack of excitement by the small business sector in Britain indicates that even substantial business allowances will not stimulate many small start-ups. It does not seem likely that relief of corporate taxes will be much more effective here. A recent NFIB survey of its urban members, for instance, asked them what were the ten greatest problems they faced when they started their companies. Raising capital was the leading problem—taxation came seventh out of ten.[12] This is not surprising. Few small, new companies created by independent entrepreneurs pay much federal tax in their first few years of operation, because they are not very profitable. So depreciation allowances, corporate tax relief, and similar business tax changes have little impact on their inclination to start a firm, or on the firm's chances of survival in the first year or so.

Relaxing the tax burden on business in the conventional way will tend to help only already growing companies, or branches of established, profitable companies that are set up in the zones. This may help younger companies to grow more quickly, by improving their cash flow, but it is unlikely to have any major effect on the

148

birthrate of firms. But accelerating the growth of firms is valuable, if it creates more employment and prosperity, and so business tax relief which encourages the expansion of small to medium-sized firms would be helpful. But there should be a low ceiling on such tax relief—it should not be extended to larger companies. David Birch and others have shown that these larger companies are just *not* the major job creators. As development consultant Paul Pryde has explained, providing such firms with tax incentives will not turn them into rapid job-generators: "Simply transferring cash to them will certainly not help them grow quickly; mature companies can't. It's like trying to make gazelles out of dinosaurs by feeding them more."[13]

Providing significant tax incentives for larger companies within Enterprise Zones also runs the risk that they will become tax havens. Creative accountants might enable corporations to achieve considerable tax savings with very little benefit for the zone neighborhood. It was the possibility of this, in fact, that discouraged the British from including any provision for a reduction in corporate income tax in their zone legislation.

For reasons such as these, the use of tax incentives for business should not be seen as a major element of the entrepreneurial climate in an Enterprise Zone. Accelerated depreciation allowances and reductions in the rate of corporate income tax should be seen only as instruments to improve the growth potential of smaller, profitable companies. There should not be a flat reduction in corporate income tax in the zones, and any relief should be confined to low levels of corporate profits. Similarly, any improved allowance against tax for new capital equipment should be confined to low total expenditures.

Since new firms are high-risk ventures, and since the risks are even higher in depressed neighborhoods, it is little wonder that traditional lending institutions steer clear of start-ups in declining areas. Most new firms obtain capital from personal savings or from affluent friends. The problem in the zones is that rich friends tend to be in short supply.

But there are ways in which the tax code might be used to overcome this problem. There are many investors in the country who are on high personal tax levels and who are willing to make high-risk investments if losses can be applied against their taxable income. Adjusting the tax code to make small companies in

149

Enterprise Zones attractive to such investors could generate a considerable flow of funds into the neighborhoods. A number of mechanisms that might achieve this have been suggested by Paul Pryde, including the following.

- *Allow investors in small zone companies to establish a loss reserve equal to (say) 20% of the capital at risk.* This would permit the individual investor to deduct part of the initial investment against his taxable income.

- *Allow all taxes on capital gains made on investments in zone firms to be deferred as long as the proceeds are reinvested in other eligible zone companies.* This would be similar to the deferment on gains made on residential property for personal use. If a limit were imposed on the total deferment that could be taken on any one investment, it would encourage capital to flow into new companies.

- *Allow zone firms to "pass through" operating losses and unused tax allowances to the investor.* Individuals can take a loss made by a company in which they invest only in the case of a narrow group of firms which qualify under Subchapter S of the Internal Revenue Code. Pryde suggests that small Enterprise Zone firms be given the same status so that allowances and losses made in the first years of a firm could be used by the investors on a pro rata basis. This might be a powerful incentive for investors to put their money into high-risk new firms.

- *Allow suppliers providing trade credit to Enterprise Zone firms more flexibility in setting up bad debt reserves.* Trade credit is usually crucial to new firms. Enabling suppliers to take a greater deduction for a bad debt reserve would encourage them to take the risk of dealing with zone firms.

If a package of this nature were incorporated as a standard feature of an Enterprise Zone, it would improve the flow of capital into new, high-risk companies. It is interesting to note that the British government, in its 1981 budget, adopted the policy of trying to stimulate new, small companies by providing *investors* with tax breaks, rather than the companies themselves. For a trial period of

150

three years, investors will be able to take up to £10,000 in additional tax relief, at their marginal tax rate, providing that it is to a single, new, independent firm (not a branch), which has been in a high-risk area for less than three years.[14]

It would be necessary to apply some safeguards in such a package, as the British are doing with their three-year experiment. There is the danger that special finance companies could develop in the zone as vehicles for tax avoidance. So the incentives would need to be structured to ensure that investment flowed into productive, job-creating firms.

It might be argued that there is very little difference between using the tax code to provide a source of private capital to new firms, and doing the same thing through "up front" loans and grants from the government. But there are important differences. In the first place, the cost to government is likely to be much lower. The cost would be confined to the *extra* tax withheld by the investor, compared with the tax savings he might achieve in some other form of tax shelter. In addition, it does not involve a monopoly of financial support, allocated by bureaucrats who have no personal stake in the ventures. It allows the entrepreneur to "shop around," and it gives even the most innovative ideas at least a chance of support. From a subjective point of view, as well as an economic one, there is also something very satisfying about providing incentives for those on high rates of personal tax—people who have made it—to invest in people who are struggling to get on the first rung of the ladder.

OPTIONAL FEDERAL ADDITIONS TO A ZONE

The package of tax changes and regulatory simplification discussed above would form the foundation of the Enterprise Zones. But if the city were prepared for more than standard concessions to match the basic package, the federal government could offer other concessions and experimental programs for the zone. These optional extras, which would be available as part of a contract, might include the following.

Foreign Trade Zone

Hundreds of cities around the world, including more than fifty in the United States, have discovered economic stimulus that can result from the creation of a foreign (free) trade zone. The foreign trade zone allows the importers to defer duties on goods until they leave the zone for the domestic market. The duties are not collected at all if the goods are reexported. The zones are therefore very attractive as sites for warehousing and transshipping facilities. In addition, the value added in a foreign trade zone can be deducted from the total duty payable on a product assembled from imported components when it enters the domestic market. This is a powerful incentive to foreign companies to establish assembly plants in order to obtain the savings in duty. Heavy foreign investment is seen in most foreign trade zones in the world. In Hong Kong, for instance, it has been estimated that as many of 60,000 jobs are due to foreign investment in the colony.[15]

A foreign trade zone could be a valuable addition to an Enterprise Zone. It would add an inflow of foreign capital to the local capital base. It could also induce some major assembly plants to locate in the inner city, providing jobs and an anchor for the local small business community. The type of labor needed by assembly factories tends to be unskilled or semiskilled—precisely the kind of labor that is plentiful in the central cities.

Housing Vouchers

Within an Enterprise Zone, the federal government might experiment with various proposals aimed at improving housing conditions in depressed areas by means of housing vouchers or similar ideas designed to enable the poor to obtain decent housing. The zones would also be appropriate as places to test proposals that could encourage rehabilitation, either through tax incentives or by a federal homesteading program. As mentioned earlier, a federal program such as this in an Enterprise Zone could be linked to a local agreement to eliminate rent control.

Reverse Income Tax

The reverse income tax proposal is only one idea that could be introduced in a zone as a possible solution to the disincentive effects inherent in the welfare system. The loss of welfare benefits involved in taking low-paid work discourages many low-skilled city residents from accepting employment—or means that they will work only in the underground economy. The reverse income tax would consolidate and simplify the welfare benefits that zone residents would receive, and soften the withdrawal of benefits when a job is taken.

Minimum Wage

The minimum wage is an emotionally charged issue, but most of the dispute over the issue concerns differing judgments of the results that would follow from a reduction or an elimination of the wage floor. Some argue that it would reduce wages for those already employed, rather than create new jobs: others claim that there would be an enormous increase in jobs if the minimum wage were removed. Given that the Enterprise Zone would be an area of very high unemployment, there would be little to lose and much to gain from testing the argument in the limited area of a zone. It would even be possible to experiment with a reduction or elimination of the minimum wage in some zones, with the agreement of the city, and a youth minimum wage in some others.

Davis-Bacon Act

The federal government could reduce or eliminate the effect of the Davis-Bacon Act in an Enterprise Zone by suitable changes in regulations or in the law itself. By requiring so-called prevailing wages to be paid on most projects involving federal money, the act has become a serious impediment to groups involved in self-help and "sweat-equity" projects aimed at rehabilitating their own neighborhoods. Eliminating the impact of the act would not only reduce the cost of renovating property but also open up more opportunities for local residents to acquire construction skills as a basis for future employment.

Pooling Insurance

The cost and difficulty of obtaining business insurance in depressed areas is a significant problem facing new companies. The very designation of an area as an Enterprise Zone may cause insurance companies to take a different view of the neighborhood, but it is still unlikely that insurance rates in the zones would fall to reasonable levels until significant development occurred. But the cost of insurance is a strong inhibitor of development. This Catch 22 situation might be eased by a system of group or pooled insurance partly underwritten either by the federal government alone or by a joint federal-local guarantee. The government already provides below-market-rate flood insurance for people in high-risk areas. One of the effects of government-supported flood insurance, however, is to encourage greater investment in an area where the risk remains the same—and so the total commitment by government increases. In depressed communities, however, the development that would occur as a result of the government-supported insurance would tend to lower the risk (through reduced crime, vandalism and fire risk), and so the government commitment would tend to fall over time.

Benefits to Zone Residents

One skepticism often expressed about the Enterprise Zone is that development might take place, entrepreneurs might make money while they create jobs, and the neighborhood might improve, but perhaps few of the residents would share in the rise of land values and other economic benefits that could accrue to those taking the lead in business. The federal government might try to deal with this reservation by experimenting with possible ways of ensuring that residents of the area obtain a direct financial benefit from development in the zone.

An interesting way in which this might be done has been suggested by the Washington-based National Center for Employee Ownership. The NCED argues that a General Stock Ownership Corporation (GSOC), created in the 1978 tax act, could be a very suitable vehicle for bringing some of the rewards of zone development directly to the residents. A state is empowered under the tax act to set up a GSOC, which then sets up a trust. All the residents of the state are stockholders, and beneficiaries, of the trust, and control it by electing trustees. The GSOC can engage in housing development or commercial enterprises, and can borrow funds in the market. The gains made by the corporation are passed to the trust and thence to the residents.

With only minor amendments to the law, the GSOC could operate in the same manner within an Enterprise Zone, with the zone residents as stockholders. In agreeing to extend the GSOC model to an Enterprise Zone on an experimental basis, the federal government might require the city to pass to the GSOC title on part, or all, of the vacant land and abandoned buildings it owns within the zone. The corporation would then have an asset that could yield lease or sale revenue for residents as property values increased and development occurred.

THE LOCAL COMMITMENT

The options discussed above are examples of what could be introduced in an Enterprise Zone if the city were prepared to make changes at its level, in cooperation with other relevant jurisdictions. The local concessions that would be sought by the federal government would deal mainly with the broad body of restrictive regulation that discourages business and neighborhood innovation. In order to obtain the basic Enterprise Zone package, a city would have to assemble a set of measures that the federal government felt were adequate for the basic tax and regulatory package. The local concessions could vary widely from zone to zone, but the common thrust would have to be that they facilitated enterprise and neighborhood innovation. If the city wished to go beyond the basic Enterprise Zone, it would have to negotiate further federal changes in the zone in return for a wider program of changes at the local level.

The elements of the local package might include the following, among others. The more radical a zone the city was prepared to contemplate, the more elements could be included.

Zoning

The city would put forward a suggested pattern of land use that would apply throughout the entire zone, without various activities being restricted to certain parts of the zone. Relaxed general rules regarding incompatible land use would protect the residents, but mixed uses would be allowed, as would the use of temporary structures. The mixed use of land is so essential to the Enterprise Zone idea that this should be given priority in zone contracts.

Building Codes

A revision of building codes within Enterprise Zones, which would allow new processes and material to be freely used, would reduce cost without reducing quality or safety levels. A city might agree to combine the streamlining of building codes with "one-stop" processing of building applications within the zone.

Alternative Services

The provision of services in many declining areas is extremely expensive, inefficient, and a City Hall monopoly. A city could agree to allow the Enterprise Zone residents to seek bids from other companies for garbage collection, fire service, and even protection and street maintenance. Those owners that contracted with private suppliers could be exempted from the appropriate proportion of local taxes.

Neighborhood Groups

Throughout the country, neighborhood organizations have shown themselves well able to provide residents with many forms of service, such as crime-watch programs, block patrols, day-care centers, homes for destitute individuals, and the like. Instead of frustrating these "unofficial" activities with local regulations aimed at regularizing and standardizing them, the city could agree as a matter of policy to keep out of their way and allow them to become a significant and valuable part of the zone neighborhood.

Neighborhood Corporations

The GSOC has already been suggested as one mechanism that might enable the residents of an Enterprise Zone to benefit as a group from the economic development that takes place. But it is only one among many possibilities. The Sabre Foundation of Washington, D.C., has suggested that there might be a general policy in Enterprise Zones whereby the ownership of city-owned land and buildings in a zone would be transferred to neighborhood organizations of various kinds. The foundation envisions the land being an important source of income to a neighborhood association, which could be used to provide job-training programs, day-care centers, small business support functions, etc. Sabre also points out that an association could reach a contract with a large corporation, under which it would lease a site in return for the provision of training programs and other assistance to the area.

In its contract with the federal government, the city might agree to facilitate the establishment of various—and possibly competing—neighborhood corporations of this type, and to provide them with tax benefits and parcels of city-owned land. A GSOC or Community Development Corporation might engage in development on behalf of all the zone residents, and provide services and start-up assistance for local businesses. Smaller neighborhood corporations might also be formed within the zone. Some of these might engage in cooperative business activity with the sole purpose of enriching the stockholders (i.e., residents). Others might use their business revenue to provide loans or inexpensive facilities for residents who wished to enter private business or form cooperatives. It would depend on the choice of the residents of the area covered by the corporation.

Rent Control

Phasing out rent control should be given priority in every Enterprise Zone. In many cities decontrol is politically impossible under the present circumstances, but in general the federal government should press hard on the issue. The short-term impact of decontrol on low-income renters can be very damaging, however. As suggested earlier, local commitment to phase out controls, in combination with an experimental federal rent-support program, could be a way of minimizing the hardship for tenants while the rental housing market adjusted to decontrol.

Homesteading and Shopsteading

Homesteading and its commercial equivalent, shopsteading, have been successful at introducing low-capital "urban pioneers" into areas where the stock of buildings is dilapidated but basically sound. Under each program, the city allows the purchaser to obtain the deed at a nominal price, providing he agrees to bring the building up to code within a specified period. And often this means with the use of his own labor. In the case of shopsteading, this usually results in business income being used to improve the property. Within an Enterprise Zone, the city might consider encouraging neighborhood corporations to provide assistance to their resident members who wished to homestead or shopstead.

Property Tax Reduction

The original Kemp-Garcia bill required cities to reduce their property taxes in the zone. This was dropped in the revised version primarily because of state constitutional reasons. But the economic arguments for a reduction in property taxes in very depressed areas remains strong. If the yield on the tax is low at the high rates that apply, and if the burden of tax is driving businesses out of the area, then lowering the rate may not only help revive business activity by reducing overhead costs, but it may actually lead to an increase in tax revenue.

Development Program

Although the Enterprise Zone concept sees government as taking the back seat in the development of the area, the city might agree as part of its contract with the federal government to make some improvements to the infrastructure of the zone. This should not be a considerable expenditure, if the emphasis is correctly on small enterprise and rehabilitation. The city might also agree to support a centerpiece development, possibly in cooperation with the federal government. But such projects should not be seen as the principal, or even as major, elements of an Enterprise Zone.

The combination of items agreed to in an Enterprise Zone contract would lead to a total package that could differ markedly from zone to zone. So it is difficult to imagine a "typical" Enterprise Zone. The process set in motion by the climate created in the zone would lead to quite different results in different places. The common thread would be the ease with which new businesses and novel social ideas could be attempted. Some people would use the opportunity afforded by the zone to start up the economic ladder and then leave the area, as people once used to do in poor but vibrant city neighborhoods. If it did that it would be a great success. As these people left, others would arrive seeking the same opportunity.

It is important to envision an Enterprise Zone in this dynamic sense. It is not a mechanism merely to reward people who happen to live in a particular place, as an end in itself. Rather, it is a device to provide concentrations of poor people with the chance of upward mobility. Change in the nature of the neighborhood over time, and in the composition of its residents, would be a characteristic of an Enterprise Zone, as it is with all strong inner-city neighborhoods.

Objections to the Enterprise Zone

In the debate over the Enterprise Zone concept in the United States, a number of conceptual criticisms have emerged. Several of these have already been addressed in this book, but it would be useful to summarize the main objections that have been raised.

Tax Sensitivity of Business

The Enterprise Zone idea must contend with a dilemma regarding tax incentives and business decisions. If, as a strong body of evidence suggests, location decisions by corporations are not strongly influenced by the tax regime in an area, then it would seem that they are unlikely to move into an Enterprise Zone.[16] If, on the other hand, companies do move to a zone, then the Enterprise Zone concept could be accused of merely robbing one neighborhood to assist another.

If the Enterprise Zone were a case of creating an environment that would cause business to relocate to depressed areas, then the dilemma would represent a serious objection. But the purpose is to create *new* economic activity. As David Birch has shown, it is the birthrate of small companies that must be improved in depressed areas. Trying to entice big companies back into depressed neighborhoods is neither feasible nor likely to be very effective.

For this reason, the tax incentives suggested for the Enterprise Zones should be geared primarily toward the problem of start-up capital, which is the principal obstacle facing would-be businessmen in depressed neighborhoods. Not only would tax incentives of this type meet the real problem, but they would also be unattractive to most large, established firms that have access to more institutional forms of finance. If the tax incentives are deepened, in order to give a significant tax benefit to existing firms, it would either have little additional effect on the number of companies appearing in the zones, or it would result in relocation from other districts. These are both good reasons *not* to aim the incentives at mature companies.

Border Effects

An issue related to relocation is the dispute over the effect of an Enterprise Zone on businesses immediately adjacent to the designated area. Small businesses in Britain have been particularly irritated by what they see as the possibility of firms on the wrong side of the border facing unfair competition from zone firms with generous tax breaks and minimal regulation.

To some degree, this effect is unavoidable. *Every* change or project hurts some people, even though the net result may be very beneficial to the community as a whole. Obviously the boundaries of an Enterprise Zone ought to be drawn in such a way as to avoid cutting through business districts. It should be remembered, of course, that the zones would not be located in places that are thriving with economic activity that could be hurt.

The border issue, however, should be seen in perspective. Urban decay is a cancerous phenomenon. Block follows block down the economic spiral. A business on the edge of a blighted area may be marginally viable today, but it lives under the shadow of depression. A firm may very probably find it difficult to raise finance, and very difficult to lure customers to the unsavory part of the city.

If the blighted district experiences a revival, thanks to the Enterprise Zone, the upward spiral would help businesses on the edge of the zone, just as the downward spiral hurts them. The zone itself might still seem unduly risky to more conservative lending institutions, but the improving strength of the zone would make existing firms on the border a better investment possibility than they once were. Such firms could also enjoy the local improvement of property values produced by activity in the zone. And the income stream created by employment in the zone would no doubt flow over into the neighboring districts.

Confining the tax breaks in an Enterprise Zone to young, start-up companies would also reduce the possibility of nearby firms being hurt by competition. If companies could grow large in an Enterprise Zone, and still enjoy major tax concessions, then it could indeed pose problems for smaller companies nearby. But if the concessions are significant only for new, small firms, the danger of that is reduced considerably.

Displacement

Some critics see the Enterprise Zone more as a threat to people in a neighborhood than as an opportunity for them. They envisage people returning from the suburbs, displacing poor inner-city residents, and pushing up rents and real estate values to the detriment of those whom the zone was supposed to help.

On one level, these critics may be asked in turn just what *would* constitute an improvement in the inner cities? If the outflow of middle-income people from an older neighborhood is damaging because it erodes the tax base and leads to stagnation, then why is it also damaging when these same people come back to the neighborhood? And if economic improvement is harmful to poor people, then presumably the best policy would be to make inner-city districts as unpleasant as possible, so that property values and rents drift even lower!

On the other hand, there is some reason to fear that the benefits of an Enterprise Zone would not necessarily flow in great measure to many of its residents. Displacement is not likely to be a major problem, since the locations will usually be places that suffer from underpopulation, but it is reasonable to ask how poor, unemployable residents would be affected, and how far we can be sure that local people will be the ones to find jobs and start new firms.

It has already been pointed out that if we are to achieve better living conditions for the residents of depressed areas then *someone* has to pay the increased cost. If that is not accepted then the poor will remain in their present squalor. If we set in motion a process that does lead to improvement, we must supplement the income of poor people to match the increase in the cost of housing. Possible ways of doing this have been discussed, and they should be employed in the Enterprise Zone.

Ensuring that residents will obtain a reasonable share of the jobs and economic prosperity in the zone may be more complicated. Congressmen Kemp and Garcia have suggested that companies obtaining tax benefits in an Enterprise Zone must recruit a specified proportion of their employees from within the zone. This is not a very satisfactory solution. As mentioned earlier, this could lead to fake addresses and just the kind of red tape that inhibits business. But if the incentives in the zone are aimed primarily at small companies, then local people will be the main beneficiaries, because of the kind of jobs they offer.

In addition, the various ideas suggested for the city-federal contract would bring direct benefits to local residents. A GSOC or

161

some other form of neighborhood corporation would ensure that residents gained from real estate and business development. Similarly, a program of shopsteading, neighborhood cooperatives, or similar city-supported ventures could have a residency requirement.

The Cost of Enterprise Zones

Calculating the cost of an Enterprise Zone depends very much on how one views the cost of a tax incentive. Some critics see any tax rate reduction as a tax loss, or "expenditure." But if the effect of reducing tax rates in an area is to create new business that would not otherwise have existed, it constitutes an increase in total tax revenue. If the zone has few businesses presently within it, there will be only a small loss to offset against the gain. The net cost of an Enterprise Zone depends on the difference between the revenue that flows into the Treasury from new companies, and the reduction in tax revenue from firms already in the zone or firms that relocate there, together with the net tax savings obtained by investors in the zone. The cost would be reduced if one took into account, as one should, the savings in welfare costs when people are provided with work.

The cost-benefit ratio of the Enterprise Zone is likely to be attractive. If the sites are restricted to areas that are heavily blighted, there is not likely to be much of a loss on existing businesses. And if the tax incentives are concentrated on small, young companies, the proportion of genuinely new enterprises will be high. The "optional extras" in some zones, such as housing vouchers or similar devices, would be additions to the basic cost. But such costs would depend very much on just how successful the Enterprise Zone became. Only if strong activity did occur, and property values rose, would expenditures on rent support and similar programs begin to rise.

The tax-incentive approach to revitalization is very different from major programs involving "up front" money. The policy of grants and loans to new companies not only involves putting public money at high risk, but it also involves a heavy commitment merely in the hope that economic activity will spring out of the rubble. When the stimulus is provided by means of a tax break, however, the Treasury "pays out" only when activity takes place. There is

162

another interesting aspect of the Enterprise Zone approach. The more depressed an area is, and the fewer businesses exist in that area, the lower will be the cost of the program if it generates new economic activity—since the loss of revenue on present activity will be very small. The economics of public expenditure on Enterprise Zones is practically the reverse of normal urban programs.

NOTES

1. Stuart Butler, *Enterprise Zones: A Solution to the Urban Crisis?* (The Heritage Foundation, Washington, D.C., 1979).
2. *Tom Stivers (ed.), The Source Book of American State Legislation* (American Legislative Exchange Council, Washington, D.C., 1980).
3. H.R. 7240.
4. H.R. 7563. An identical version of the bill was introduced in the Senate by Senators Boschwitz and Chafee. For a summary and analyis of the bill, see Stuart Butler, *The Urban Jobs and Enterprise Zone Act* (The Heritage Foundation, Washington, D.C., 1980).
5. *Dun's Review*, February 1981, p. 55.
6. George Sternlieb, *Kemp-Garcia Act: An Initial Evaluation* (Rutgers University, New Brunswick, N.J., 1980).
7. *Dun's Review*, February 1981, p. 55.
8. Public Law 96-354. For an analysis of the law, see Milton Stewart, "The New Regulatory Flexibility Act," *American Bar Association Journal*, January 1981.
9. Section 2(a)(3). These small units are termed "small entities" under the act.
10. Although the act requires that a "substantial" number of entities must be affected before the act comes into play, the House Report on the bill stressed that this should be considered on a case-by-case basis, and that for businesses the number affected could be as low as fifteen and the act would be triggered.
11. *Baltimore Sun*, 12 January 1981.
12. Unpublished survey, NFIB, Washington, D.C., 1981.
13. *Washington Post*, 2 March 1981.
14. *The Economist*, 14 March 1981, p. 61.
15. *Journal of Commerce*, 22 October 1979.
16. See Roger Vaughan, *The Urban Impacts of Federal Policies: Volume II, Economic Development* (Rand Corporation, Santa Monica, Calif., 1977); Roger Schmenner, *The Manufacturing Location Decision* (MIT Press, Cambridge, Mass., 1978); Bennett Harrison and Sandra Kanter, "The Political Economy of States' Job Creation Business Incentives," *AIP Journal*, October 1978.

CONCLUSION

The Enterprise Zone concept marks a radical departure in thinking on the problems of the inner cities. It is an optimistic approach, resting on the assumption that there is far more potential in even the most depressed neighborhoods than many would have us believe. We know that there can be quite dramatic results when neighborhood groups take the lead in pulling an area together. We know also, from history—and from other countries—that apparently unsophisticated people can and do succeed as entrepreneurs when they have the incentive to try. We can even see economic activity in the areas we are trying to revive— and not just criminal activity. In some areas, there is a strong underground economy where services and goods are provided for cash.

The Enterprise Zone recognizes this. As Jack Kemp once remarked, inside every moonlighter there is a small businessman trying to get out. The reason he usually stays underground in the inner city is that in such a hostile environment, the additional costs and bother of establishing a legitimate business are simply too great. And so instead of setting up a firm and employing some local people, the talented entrepreneur takes the easier road and does not grow. The Enterprise Zone would clear away some of the costs and red tape that stand in the way of the enterprising local citizen.

Reducing tax and regulatory burdens in order to increase the rate of new business start-ups in the inner city would be a wise investment for the Treasury. Killing the golden goose may seem a singularly inappropriate metaphor when speaking of blighted neighborhoods. But in such areas the complexity and tax costs of going into business, on top of all the other problems, discourage many potential taxpayers from even considering legitimate business. Reducing the burdens on new firms means that taxpayers of the future are created.

The emphasis in the Enterprise Zone on new, small firms is crucial for the many reasons discussed earlier. But two are of particular importance in the long term. Creating new businesses means adding to the economy rather than redistributing it. It means enabling people in one place to use what they have more effectively to improve their own situation. This is important because the Enterprise Zone should not be confused with policies that aim to lure companies from one place to another, or to the benefit of one group of people and the detriment of another. If we can create an environment in which the residents of the South Bronx, or Newark, or Liberty City are given the incentive to pull themselves up by their own efforts, then the policy is defensible. If we simply provide them with jobs taken from somewhere else in the country it would be hard to justify, whatever improvement we see in the depressed parts of the major cities.

The second long-term reason for the emphasis on small business start-ups is that the Enterprise Zone sees the creation of a strong local business class as essential for a sustained improvement. Most programs think only in terms of giving major employers an incentive to come into a neighborhood and employ local people. The Enterprise Zone, on the other hand, is what one might call a "trickle-up" approach to economic development—local people starting in modest jobs and businesses and moving slowly up the ladder.

The Enterprise Zone does not guarantee success to anyone, even though it reduces some of the unnecessary causes of failure. Implicit in the concept is the sacred right of all Americans to lose money in business. Although it may be justly argued that people in blighted areas can little afford to lose, the reply may be that by removing barriers and costs, the Enterprise Zone keeps the stakes as low as possible. But risks must remain for, together with the prospect of profit, risk concentrates the mind of every entrepreneur.

The Enterprise Zone would give people greater control over their lives. When individuals (or communities) are allowed to make decisions for themselves, they respond to the challenge. As businessmen they are more creative and they will work harder and longer. When neighborhood organizations are given the freedom to develop their own ideas, rather than having to petition and persuade City Hall, they tend to be more enthusiastic and successful. They know the local circumstances and they have a commitment to the project which is understandably absent in an outsider.

It may be argued that if the Enterprise Zone is seen as such an effective tool, then why ration it? Why not create an Enterprise Zone coast to coast? While such sentiments are reasonable on their face, there are good reasons for choosing a more limited approach. In the first place, not everyone by any means is convinced that the zones will be beneficial. Even if the elements of the Enterprise Zone are indeed suitable for every location, there would be fierce, and probably successful, opposition to such a radical change for the whole country. In highly depressed neighborhoods, however, there is very little to lose; there can be general agreement to try something quite new. We would be replacing only things that had failed in these areas, not things that have been successful. Nevertheless, the Enterprise Zone would be a demonstration of the effectiveness of policies designed to unshackle enterprise and local creativity. If the demonstration proved successful, there would be good cause to extend elements of the idea, or the entire mechanism, across the country.

The second reason for a program limited to depressed urban neighborhoods is that, although the substantial dismantling of government restrictions and taxation may be an inexpensive and highly beneficial approach to blighted areas, the same action may be less successful elsewhere. In places with a very strong local economy, significant tax reduction could involve a heavy loss of revenue to the Treasury. Similarly, settled and stable residential areas may feel that streamlining federal and local regulations would remove protection without bringing many tangible advantages. Although the broad approach of stimulating new activity by reducing government obstacles may be a valuable guide to policy, the most radical version of the approach is best suited to places where the need is greatest.

It would be wrong, therefore, to think of the Enterprise Zone as a general urban policy. In the first place it is an extreme solution to an extreme situation in certain neighborhoods. But we can, of course, learn things of general application from a limited program. We may find successes that would suggest changes in general policy. We may also see ways in which the basic approach may be applied to other, but still limited, types of location. A rural version of the concept, aimed at small towns, is already under consideration. Another possibility worth examining would be a city-wide zone designed to accelerate the recovery of a city which is suffering the decline of the industry that once dominated it. If we could create in Detroit, for instance, an environment in which thousands of new small firms were encouraged to try out new processes and ideas, we would build a secure economic foundation for the city much more rapidly than by providing any amount of government aid to the chosen few.

Not only is the Enterprise Zone not a general policy, but it is also not a replacement for government policies that work—only for those that have failed. In its purest form, it is something well worth trying in areas that seem beyond hope—where it seems pointless to invest government money. In other places, the Enterprise Zone may be seen as forming the base for other policies. A training program, for instance, is far more likely to achieve results when new jobs are also being created. Similarly, a zone would lead to the more rapid creation of businesses linked to a UDAG or similar government project. An Enterprise Zone creates a climate that could enhance the effectiveness of government programs, as well as private sector programs.

Jack Kemp has often referred to the Enterprise Zone as "greenlining" the inner city. Both he and Robert Garcia understand well that perhaps the greatest problem depressed areas actually face is that the strengths of the neighborhoods are not appreciated, and that government often restricts activity rather than encourages it. Cities have to find all the things that are *wrong* with their neighborhoods if they are to receive support from government; people are forced to talk things down in order to qualify for cash and projects. Is it any wonder that when we make such people act like paupers they begin to *think* like paupers, and assume the only way to survive is to demand help from others?

Greenlining the inner cities, in the form of the Enterprise Zone, means providing an environment in which people have an incentive to think in terms of strengths rather than weaknesses, and to look for opportunities rather than handouts. Such a climate once

167

characterized great cities and made them centers of innovation and optimism. It enabled them to adapt to economic change and to prosper from it. But we have slowly eradicated the spirit of innovation by stifling it with government restrictions and taxation. The Enterprise Zone is a way of recreating that spirit in the most depressed urban areas.

INDEX

abandonment, 21, 38, 39, 46, 47, 135 (*see also* housing)
Adam Smith Institute, 98
American Legislative Exchange Council, 130
Amsterdam News, 49
apartments (*see* housing)
Armstrong, William, 40
Association of Independent Businesses (AIB, Britain), 121–23

"balloon frame" houses, 3
Baltimore, 9, 10, 18, 27, 28, 32, 64, 78, 142
Belmont district (Bronx, N.Y.), 87–88
Birch, David, 66–67, 77–79, 92, 120, 149, 159
Birmingham (Britain), 83–84
Boorstin, Daniel, 2, 3, 3n
borrowing, 29, 64–67, 151
Boston, 9, 10, 26, 28, 32–34, 78
Bradley, Thomas, 142
Bronx, N.Y., 4–5, 44, 47, 48, 60, 87–88, 138, 165
Buffalo, N.Y., 11, 17, 18, 28
building codes: 137; criticism of, 51, 52, 53, 56; defined, 51 (*see also* deregulation; zoning)
businesses: attitude of city government, 60–61; new ventures, 81–82; retail and service firms, 11–12; small businessmen, 76, 81, 82; small business sector, 13, 14, 57, 76–77, 85 (*see also* manufacturing)
Business Week, 63

Capitol Hill, 10
Carter, Jimmy, 19, 63
Carter Administration, 63
Census (1980), 7
Census Bureau, 8, 9, 10, 41, 44
CETA, 70–71
Chafee, John, 134
Chicago, 8, 28, 64
Chisholm, Shirley, 70
cities, 1–9, 14–20, 164–68 (*see also* neighborhoods; suburbs)
city finances: borrowing, 29; boundary taxation, 25; city services costs, 15; expenditures, 18; revenue, 26–28 (*see also* taxes)
Cleveland, 8–9, 17, 18, 28
Clydebank (Britain), 111, 114, 115
Columbia, Maryland, 31
Commerce, U.S. Department of, 29, 134
Commission for a National Agenda, 19–20
"community": Belmont district (Bronx, N.Y.), 87–88; community leaders, 90–91; North End (Boston), 34; South Boston, 34
Community Development Block Grants (CDBG), 62

171

income: 161; decline among city residents, 9; transfer payments, 9–10 (*see also* low-income; middle-income)
industry (*see* businesses; manufacturing)
Isle of Dogs (Britain), 1, 99

Jacobs, Jane, 2, 32–33, 56, 82–85, 108, 124
jobs: 11, 92, 100–101, 108–09; employment creation, 75–77, 80, 139–41, 162; in private sector, 16, 76; in small business sector, 57–59, 85, 120, 127, 140–41, 159–60; training programs, 71; unemployment, 67–70 (*see also* labor; unemployment)
Joint Economic Committee of Congress, 58, 61
Jones, Roscoe, 56–57
Joseph, Sir Keith, 98–99

Kemp, Jack, 131, 133, 136, 138, 161, 164, 167
Kemp-Garcia Urban Jobs and Enterprise Zone Act, 131 (*see also* Enterprise Zones in America)
Koch, Edward, 46, 138, 142

labor: mobility, 20–21, 25–26; skilled, 8, 13, 25, 134; unskilled, 8, 14, 58, 64, 70, 83, 134, 152 (*see also* jobs; unemployment)
Labor, U.S. Department of, 35
Labour Party (Britain), 113–14
landlords (*see* housing; rent control; tenants)
Levitt, Arthur, 58
Lewis, Evan, 114
Liberty City, 71, 140, 165
Lindbeck, Assar, 44
Local Government Planning and Land Act (Britain, 1980), 103
London, 20, 84
Long, Larry, 10
Los Angeles, 8, 50, 53, 84
low-income, 33–35, 43–45, 55–57, 161 (*see also* income; middle-income)

maintenance, 46–48 (*see also* "deferred maintenance")
Manchester (Britain), 8, 13, 84, 111, 115–16
manufacturing: decline of traditional industry, 12; high technology industry, 12, 96; new patterns, 13, 95–96; single–industry cities, 84; small manufacturing, 60 (*see also* businesses)
Mestres, Jean, 85
middle–income, 17, 33, 34, 45, 161 (*see also* income; low–income)
Midwest, 7, 27
migration (*see* population movements)
minimum wage, 67–69, 71, 130, 136, 142, 153
mobility, 20
Model Cities program, 125
Motley, John, 136
multi–zone, 119
Myrdal, Gunnar, 49

172

173

174

Swansea (Britain), 111, 114–18